Simple Prayer

Simple Prayer

John Dalrymple

DARTON·LONGMAN + TODD

This edition published in 2010 by
Darton, Longman and Todd Ltd
1 Spencer Court
140–142 Wandsworth High Street
London SW18 4JJ

First published 1984

ISBN: 978-0-232-52779-7

A catalogue record for this book is available from the British Library.

Phototypeset by Kerrypress Ltd, Luton, Bedfordshire
Printed and bound in Great Britain by Cromwell Press Group,
Trowbridge, Wiltshire

For

Michael

il miglior fabbro

Contents

Foreword

There was a time, which still lasts in some parts of Scotland, when Protestants who wanted to learn something about spirituality would swallow their denominational pride and try to entice a Roman Catholic priest or nun to address them.

This is how I met Jock Dalrymple. It was around 1981, the time when he was working on talks which would become the content of this book. I asked him to come to Glasgow and speak to an adult Christian education class. He readily assented, and what he said – as I realised on re-reading *Simple Prayer* – changed my life for good.

There have been many people of Jock Dalrymple's intellect and deep piety who have written for others. But often they have drawn so much on their own clerical or academic experience and punctuated their writing with so many obtuse quotes from spiritual giants, that the average reader is made to feel personally inadequate and in awe of the author.

But not here. For in *Simple Prayer* we are enabled, through clear and affectionate language, to be drawn into a fond yearning for God. And God is never referred to as a religious formula it will take a lifetime to understand, but as one who must be known as person to person or not at all. Spirituality is both mystical and relational, but it is not the sole preserve of a select few, as the humbling postscript makes clear.

Here, some things are said in language so direct that it is a glorious relief to read what we may have longed to hear: 'We have to be prepared, calmly and deliberately, to be incompetent at prayer,' or, 'There is no point in persevering with a (spiritual) book which is not helping us to pray.' But undergirding this and many other helpful insights is the valuing of kindness from and for God which is the primary context on which our devotional life depends.

I remember listening first of all in disbelief, and then in new-born conviction as Jock, in speaking of his own prayer life to the audience in Glasgow, said with wonderful sincerity.

'Sometimes I just sit quietly, and after a while I say, "I love you, God. I love you, God." And I might say it over and over again. Nothing else. And then I dare to hear what I believe God is also saying, "I love you, Jock. I love you, Jock." '

Time has neither jaded my memory of that salutary moment, nor has it made redundant any of the ever fresh truths in *Simple Prayer*.

John L. Bell
The Iona Community
January 2010

Introduction

I have spent much of my life promoting simple prayer as well as trying to practise it. I was led to it early on in my student days in the 1940s and have tried to remain faithful ever since. It has been the abiding pursuit of my life. Interestingly, this pursuit has led me often to be out of step with the predominant movements in the Church as I have lived out my priesthood. In the 1950s, my desire for simple, personal prayer made me dissatisfied with the impersonal scholastic theology which was the prevailing diet of my seminary days. It seemed to be full of 'things' like Grace, Merit, Satisfaction, and almost devoid of the love of a personal God which I was encountering in prayer. There was, in fact, no food for prayer in the theology I was taught. Prayer existed alongside but seemed unconnected with one's study of theology. After ordination, in parish work, I was equally disappointed with the canonical and legalistic categories within which we priests were expected to exercise our pastorate. I found that so often mediating the love and mercy of God to people meant breaking the existing rules. This was not a happy state of affairs.

Then came Vatican II and the Church's return to the Bible's presentation of a personal God in love with his creatures. Life in the Church became much more human and potentially prayerful. Vatican II was, however, immediately followed by a great wave of secularist thinking on both sides of the Atlantic. The whole idea of personal prayer and contemplation was called into question by books like Harvey Cox's 'Secular City' and the death of God theologians. Anyone who tried to set aside time for prayer apart from activity was regarded as sadly out of date. As the 1960s gave way to the 1970s, the pendulum swung away from this secularist denial of prayer to the other extreme of charismatic renewal. Suddenly prayer became the thing that mattered most, and some of those who had previously ridiculed prayer now became its articulate supporters. Prayer groups sprung up all over the place. There was a great release of the Spirit in the Church, inspiring people to pray as never before. But the prayer so enthusiastically embraced was for the most part extrovert, wordy and extravagant. It was not the simple silent prayer of contemplation.

Now we are in the 1980s and the predominant mood of the Church has moved away from those intensely personal movements like Charismatic Renewal, Marriage Encounter, Cursillo, towards more concern about global issues, in particular the clamant problem of Nuclear Armaments. Prophecy has come into its own, with the possibility that Christians may have to become non-conformists in society, even to the extent of martyrdom. While I rejoice that the prophetic element in the Church has come alive, I still find myself seeing the gospel not as an ethical matter, but one of new relationships of prayer and love: Father to sons and daughters, neighbour to neighbour. I see a danger in our new mood of moralism that the gospel of Jesus may be turned into an ethic. The New Testament teaching on salvation by faith may become obscured once more by the over-activism of human beings who see salvation in terms of what they must do for God and the world rather than in terms of what God has done for them. Only in prayer do we maintain the right proportion of things. Only by prayer will the Church remain faithful to its Master. I am grateful to the Rev. Tom Cuthill who asked me in the winter of 1981 to give a series of talks on prayer in the St Cuthbert's Centre, Edinburgh, which formed the nucleus of this book. Norah Smith and Basil Postlethwaite made valuable suggestions when the book was in manuscript. Sister Clare of Jesus did the typing and proof-reading with characteristic efficiency.

The quotation from 'The Indian Upon God' is reproduced from *Collected Poems of W. B. Yeats* by permission of Michael Yeats and Macmillan London Ltd.

Prayer Becomes Simple

1

Towards Simplicity

This is a book about personal prayer, the prayer in which, unsupported by any group, we face God on our own. It is, I think, the commonest prayer of all. Jesus, we know from the gospels, practised it much. This book aims to help the reader to understand what happens when this adventure of prayer is seriously undertaken and allowed to unfold.

Where does prayer begin? Surely by asking. 'Ask and you shall receive.' Jesus encouraged us to begin there. It is what everyone instinctively understands prayer to be: asking, interceding, beseeching God for things we want. The Old and New Testaments are full of instruction to do this. The psalms, for instance, give many examples of how to pray this prayer, because we never outgrow the needs which give rise to it. We never cease to depend on God for everything, however mystical our prayer may later become. Furthermore we *ought* never to outgrow the prayer of petition, because it is an exercise of faith in God. If you have no faith, praying to God to give you things is senseless. But with faith, it is eminently sensible.

The prayer of petition leads to the prayer of thanksgiving. When God answers prayer we turn to him in thanksgiving. Human beings being what they are, however, we are often less urgent in thanking God for things than we are in asking him for them. We readily think of God when we want things, but tend to forget him when we have no demands. This is a pity, because there is in fact no time when we cannot be thanking God, simply because he is the author of all that is best in life, the good things of this world, human company, our very existence, not to mention the supernatural life of grace. Here again the psalms show us the way. They are replete with beautiful prayers of thanksgiving for the good things God gives men and especially for his friendship, love and mercy.

> 'My soul give thanks to the Lord,
> All my being bless his holy name.
> My soul give thanks to the Lord
> And never forget all his blessings.'

(Ps 102)

Or the beautiful psalm 135 which enumerates all the blessings of creation and redemption which God has wrought for the Israelites in delivering them from the slavery of Egypt. Its opening stanza goes:

> 'O give thanks to the Lord for he is good,
> for his love endures for ever.
> Give thanks to the God of gods,
> for his love endures for ever.
> Give thanks to the Lord of lords,
> for his love endures for ever.'

It is a deeply Christian prayer.

A third form of prayer is discovered when we develop an approach to God which not only thinks of him as the source of benefits but also recognizes that we have duties towards him. This is the prayer of contrition, or sorrow for sin. In the developed conscience it comes as naturally as asking for good things. It is natural to discover that we do not succeed as we ought in pleasing God, that we fall short in our conduct and commit sins. So we turn to God and say we are sorry. We apologize to God for our behaviour and ask him to help us do better in the future. Saying sorry to God for our sins is the third basic approach to God in prayer. The penitential psalms, composed long before Christ, are still among the best expressions of this prayer, used continually in the liturgy of the Church.

The fourth approach to God is simply to forget about ourselves, both our needs and our sorrows, and turn to God and praise him. This is the purest prayer of all, because it is unmixed with the element of self. We do not pray for anything for ourselves. We praise and thank God just for being himself. God is God. Hallowed be his name! We join in the chorus of praise that goes up from creation to the Creator. The reader will not have to be told that the psalms and canticles of both Old and New Testaments are among the finest expressions of this sentiment.

> 'Praise the Lord for he is good;
> sing to our God for he is loving,
> To him our praise is due.'

(Ps 146)

That is the general refrain of all the praising psalms (cf. especially Psalms 144–150). God is God, so praise him!

I think that under these headings of Petition, Thanksgiving, Sorrow, Praise, all of prayer can be summed up. Later, as we shall see, these four approaches tend to coalesce into the general one of communion with God; but the four elements are always present in man's approach to God, though at times now one, now another, is to the fore, depending on the circumstances of the person who prays. It is important to notice that the hidden agenda of all four basic approaches is a deep recognition of the sovereignty of God. We would neither ask God for favours nor thank him, unless we believed him to be Sovereign Lord. In fact, in petitioning and thanking God we simultaneously acknowledge him as Lord. This means that even 'primitive' prayers which ask God for food, fine weather, happy holidays, are basically prayers of adoration and dependence and union with God by petitioning him. Jesus was petitioning his Father right up to the end of his life.

* * * * *

An exciting thing happens when we move closer to God in prayer by making our recognition of the sovereignty of God no longer implicit in our prayers but explicit. We make it the very business of prayer. We turn to God and make God himself the agenda of our prayer! It is no longer some business between us and God: asking for a favour, thanking him, saying sorry for our sins – which occupies us. It is God himself. We simply face God and dwell on him, his presence here and now, without further ado. We dwell on God as a Reality in our midst. We are engaged with him. And, of course, he is engaged with us. There is nothing in between. It is a direct encounter both ways. This is a step forward from asking God for things or thanking him. It is a step towards intimacy.

Intimacy in prayer comes when we find that we can remain in communion with God without any particular desire to move on to some business with him. We are content just to stay with God, conscious that he loves us, trying to respond with our own love. We dwell with God, and he with us. It is difficult to put into words what happens when prayer simplifies like this. One reason for this is that there is a progression towards wordless silence in prayer, and silence is not easy to speak about. Progress in intimacy becomes progress towards silence. This happens in all human friendship, and the divine friendship of prayer follows a similar pattern.

When strangers meet, their only form of communication is by words. They have to speak, because between strangers silence is a breakdown in communication. So at first a rather frantic and (superficial) exchange of words takes place; it is not at all relaxing because of the fear that gaps of silence may come along and spoil the conversation; nor is it communicative because strangers for all their chatter of words do not risk talking about themselves in a revealing way. They prefer to stay with safe superficialities. But if, after time, two strangers become friends, then a transformation takes place in their conversation. They begin to be able to talk about their real, deeper selves. They also begin to be able to be silent with each other, for they discover that between friends silence is not a breakdown in communication, but an alternative form of communication. Thus, friends may go for a walk together and at the end of the walk they could not say how much they had talked and how much they had been silent, because all the time, silent or talking, they had been communicating. They had shared the time together without bothering too much about conversation except when they felt like it. To get as far as this with people is extremely relaxing. It is the most enjoyable mark of friendship.

Prayer, our communication with God, follows the same pattern. There comes a time in prayer – in my experience it comes early for most people – when we find that it is possible to pray without words in a silent, wordless communion. We find we are no longer strangers with God, and need not look in a frantic fashion for words to fill the period of praying, but be quite relaxed in silence, speaking when we want to (like those two friends walking together), but also able to be silent and still in communion with the Lord. In a later chapter we will see that there is nothing surprising about this growth towards intimacy with God, since the theology of grace tells us that intimacy with God is his gift to every baptized person. It ought to be surprising when people do *not* grow towards this intimacy, not when they do. Yet the tradition in the Church for many years has been that silent, wordless prayer is achieved by only a few after much effort. It is, I think, a false tradition.

To conclude the chapter I do not want to give the impression that the move to wordless prayer with God is all plain sailing. It is often hard enough with human beings to risk the intimacy of friendship. It is harder with God because we cannot see or touch him. The whole exercise of prayer is an exercise of faith. We take it on trust that God is there and is as loving as the New Testament says he is. To the fear of becoming intimate with another, which most of us have, is added the fear of making ourselves ridiculous by spending time in silence 'with nobody'. Somehow to spend that time talking is easier and more reassuring. To be silent is more of a risk. There is also the fear of being bored if we try to be wordless in prayer. Fear of boredom often keeps us at the chattering stage with God. We keep boredom at bay with lots of words and formulas. Instinctively we are afraid that silence may lead to emptiness, even when with our minds we know that sharing God's presence can never be empty. It is good to face these rather humdrum fears at the outset of a life of prayer, because they are felt by most people and certainly real. No one will get very far in prayer unless he or she makes the initial step to face and overcome these beginners' fears. Once faced, they lose much of their power, and the road ahead is cleared to a shared intimacy with God in prayer.

2

To Know God

One way of overcoming the fear of contemplative prayer is to understand the difference between knowing about God and knowing him. We feel safe knowing about God, but not so safe when we move to knowing him.

Knowing about God, which is called meditation, is the process of reading and thinking about God and his dealings with us. A classic way to begin is to take a passage from the gospel in the life of Jesus and apply oneself to extracting a message from it for one's own life. This is a very fruitful exercise, one, surely, that should be part of every serious Christian's life. The gospels are written for our use, to help us follow Christ, be his disciples, in our own time and society. A good sermon should be a practical meditation on the New Testament applied to the lives of the hearers. The feature of this approach to God is that essentially it is talking to oneself (or a congregation) about God. One is using the imagination and the mind to reach conclusions about Jesus and apply them to one's life. One is in contact with oneself about God, but not yet in direct contact with God.

To know God is another kind of exercise. It is to move into direct contact with God, address him, be in communion with him. It is essentially different from meditating about God, the difference being that between being closed and being open. Thinking about God in prayer is a closed circuit exercise, beginning and ending with oneself. Knowing God, or 'thinking God,' is an open circuit affair, which begins with oneself but terminates at the mystery we call God. One opens oneself to the Lord in direct and mysterious contact. He is present and one is 'at his mercy' in direct encounter.

Here again in order to understand prayer it is helpful to look at the way we relate to our fellow human beings. We can know about people we have never met. It is not necessary to meet someone to know about him. That, for instance, is how most of us know our public figures. We can build up an impressive amount of knowledge about them from newspapers, books, television appearances, even perhaps from people who have met them. This knowledge can grow through years of research until it is full and accurate; but at the end of the day it remains impersonal and from a distance. In order for it to become personal, knowing rather than knowing about, we have first of all to meet that person; then we have to spend time with him, because one meeting is in no way enough for knowledge and friendship to be established; lastly, as we get to know him, he gets to know us, because we cannot say we know a person who does not at the same time know us. To say I know a friend is to say that we know each other. Personal knowledge is a sharing relationship which goes both ways.

This is what happens in prayer when we pass from knowing about God (meditation) to knowing him (contemplation). The move means that I have encountered God directly in 'open circuit' prayer, that we have spent time together (contemplation does not grow instantaneously but is a slow, persevered-in relationship), and that I come to realize more and more that in prayer God is knowing me, has in fact known me through and through from the beginning of my existence. Contemplative prayer is a sharing exercise, a wonderful exchange between Creator and creature, with nothing in between.

We are now in a position, I think, to understand why many are afraid of the advance into contemplative prayer from meditation. There are two features about this simple prayer of knowing God which can be frightening. The first is that in such prayer we are no longer in control of what happens. As long as I stay with meditation, I am in control. I look at the evidence, ask questions, form conclusions, draw applications for my life. In all this I am in charge, like any scientist or thinker examining a question. I get a certain satisfaction from conducting the business to a conclusion. Furthermore it is right that I should be in control, otherwise I would not be pursuing the matter seriously. When, however, I move to direct, simple prayer, I am no longer in charge. God is. I open myself to him, more often than not wordlessly, and deliberately hand myself over to him. I deliberately lose control and leave things to God. There is no question of pursuing a line of thought to a conclusion. I am staying still, held by the reality of God, present before me. It is not a matter of discursive thought, but of a personal surrender to God in my heart and soul. As we saw above, this silent surrender holds many understandable and legitimate fears for us. Nobody likes to surrender to someone else, least of all when it is done in faith, with no tangible evidence, to an unseen God.

The other feature of contemplative prayer is that it requires sheer faith to do it. I do not say that there is no faith required to meditate about God, but it is an undoubted fact that one can think about God, talk about him, form conclusions, without actually believing in his existence! This is how agnostics and atheists behave towards the idea of God. They, in all seriousness, conduct a sort of meditation on the possibility of his existence and nature. It is clearly different for the believer who meditates, for he or she has faith that God exists and reads the gospels in the light of that faith. Nevertheless, meditating about God does not call for faith or commitment in the way that contemplation does. It does not engage the deeper part of self which is activated by encounter with God. It is more a process of the reasoning powers than of the heart in faith. Contemplative prayer requires faith from start to finish, faith first of all that God is there, the compassionate Father that Jesus spoke about; then a generous faith to make contact and to surrender to God who is richly present but invisible. Anyone who in a busy life has set aside time to pray, knows that it calls for a lot of faith to stay at prayer in an attitude of surrender, when so many more visible things are calling for our attention. Meditating about the things of God at least has results in the form of conclusions about God and one's own life; but contemplation does not have even those results. We make our contact with God in faith and what follows we leave to God to understand, without much understanding ourselves. It is very much an exercise of the heart in love and trust without too much satisfaction for the reasoning powers.

Two well-known pieces of sculpture from the modern era illustrate for me the difference between meditation and contemplation. The first is Rodin's *Thinker*. Here is an almost perfect image of a man in deep thought, looking into himself, the position of the arms and bent legs suggesting a closed circle. The statue breathes the spirit of thought turned in on itself, somehow apart from the surroundings, perfectly recollected inwardly. The other statue is Epstein's *Jacob and the Angel*, where we see the primitive masculine figure locked in a muscular embrace with an equally primitive angel. It is another almost perfect image of what we mean by encounter. The figure of Jacob is fully engaged with the other. His prayer is one of struggle and encounter. Even the sexual overtones of the figure need not worry us when we remember that for the Hebrews to know someone meant sometimes sexual coupling. 'Eternal life is knowing thee the one true God, and Jesus Christ whom thou hast sent' (John 17:3). In the simple prayer of meeting God we are led to a complete engagement of our selves with him. Contemplation is essentially relational, an opening of ourselves to the other who is God. In prayer we bump up against God, and he against us. It may sometimes be struggle and sometimes be sweet surrender. It is always direct meeting.

3

Receptivity

True prayer is relational, a sharing of love and knowledge between the soul and God, as we saw in the last chapter. We must not, however, forget that it is a sharing between complete unequals. God and I are not equals, however much I may be elevated by his grace into a partnership with him. A good image of the true relationship between God and ourselves is that used by Jeremiah: the potter and the clay (Jer 18:1–11). God is the potter – we are clay in his hands, to do with us whatever he wills. During prayer this relationship of moulder to moulded becomes most actual. God shapes us to his purposes. All we have to do is to be receptive and let whatever God wants to happen, happen. 'And the vessel he was making of clay was spoiled in the potter's hand, and he reworked it into another vessel, as it seemed good to the potter to do. Then the word of the Lord came to me: "O house of Israel, can I not do with you as this potter has done?" says the Lord' (vv.4–5).Receptivity in God's hands is the heart of simple prayer. Here a difficulty arises for many of us, and it is wise to recognize it. Many people who will read this book are professionally trained in one way or another. The essence of professional training, be it that of teacher, lawyer, priest, social worker, business person, is that we are trained to be on top of our job, trained to cope with any eventuality, any emergency that might happen. The good teacher, for instance, has to have control of her class, and she does this by knowing both her pupils and her subject fully; furthermore much of her effectiveness comes from her ability to anticipate the future and be ready for it. She is, in other words, thoroughly in control of both present and future.

The danger is that those who have this readiness to cope with job, family, friends, may turn to prayer and unconsciously, using the same technique, try to cope with God! Not a few such persons have run up against a block in prayer precisely for this reason. They have seen the need for prayer and approached it, as they have approached other problems in their life, with a determination to be competent. They have started to master prayer but have found to their disappointment that it does not proceed by mastery. Often they have then given up in disappointment. They need to remember the potter and the clay. In prayer we are the clay, not the potter, God does the moulding and coping, not us. We have to 'change gear' at the beginning of prayer and deliberately let drop all desire to be in charge, to know where we are going, to master the situation. This is not easy for modern men and women, trained as we are to handle complicated situations and survive. The downtrodden and pushed about in life can pray without having to change gear – their situation in life is that they are clay already. But we, who are instinctive potters, have to make this deliberate renunciation of being in charge when we begin our prayer. We have to be prepared, calmly and deliberately, to be incompetent at prayer, leaving all the competence to God. For a 20th century person contemplation is not easy. 'Thou mastering me God!' How easy it is to voice that sentiment along with the poet. But it is difficult in practice to pray that sentiment and *really* allow ourselves to be mastered, resisting the temptation to tackle prayer like all our other tasks by setting out to master it.

Sometimes writers and preachers on prayer use the term 'passive' to describe the attitude before God which has been outlined in the last few paragraphs. I do not think that is a good term to use. I prefer the word 'receptive'. To be passive in the hands of God does not do justice to our humanity nor our status as children of God. A stone is passive in someone's hand: it will go where it is thrown or dropped. That does not express how we should be in God's hands. In the sense of leaving the initiative to God we have to be passive; but we have to be fully active in cooperating with what God does with us. We are called to be partners with God in the act of prayer, with a partnership of mind, heart and soul, using our humanity to the full. Such an active passivity, the attitude of the attentive listener, not the sleeper, is, I think, best described by the word receptivity. In God's hands, at prayer, we have to allow ourselves to be receptive, letting go all plans and worries, all schemes and programmes, and trusting him to mould us to his purposes. When prayer is over we will begin again to cooperate actively with those purposes, but during the time of prayer our intimate love of God should express itself in surrender, while after prayer that intimate love expresses itself in active and intelligently planned work according to the will of God.

It will now be clear that the part of our mind which is engaged in contemplative prayer is not the active intelligence which masters data and makes plans for future action. It is the intuitive faculty which takes in what is before it, without reasoning, 'at a glance' and then is content to savour the information at length. The active mind is at home in the world of 'See: Judge: Act.' The intuitive mind dwells in the presence of its object and enjoys it. We use words like 'look,' 'listen,' 'wait' for this exercise: simple exercises which do not appear to be very active but which in fact engage the whole person – the birdwatcher observing a nest perfectly still but fully alert, the mother lovingly waiting for a sick child to wake up.

Is it the mind or heart which we are talking about in this discussion? The answer is both. In contemplative prayer the mind is certainly engaged. Contrary to popular misunderstanding, in prayer the mind is not empty but full – too full of the richness of God to want to analyse, just content to dwell in wonder, like the eye dazzled by light. (So beware advice which tells us to empty the mind in prayer. We should empty it of mundane things, but only in order to fill it with God.) But, as well as the mind, the heart also is engaged in prayer, for the object before us in prayer is not impersonal facts to be mastered, but the living reality of the personal God who looks on us in love and calls us to him. We respond to that call not just with the assenting mind, but with full hearts. Prayer, then, becomes increasingly an act of love, in which we surrender to God with our whole selves. This is another reason for avoiding the word passivity. Faced with the reality of God, called by him in love, we respond with our whole being, fully active, though during the time of prayer, tranquil and still. John Henry Newman's motto, adopted when he became a cardinal, expresses well what simple prayer is: '*Cor ad cor loquitur.*' Heart speaks to heart. In simple, familiar silence we communicate with God, and he with us. There is a mutual sensitivity between creature and Creator, which passes beyond words and can only properly be understood by experiencing it.

Prayer is sometimes understood and talked about, even advertised, as an Experience. In the search for meaning to existence, contemplation is put forward as an experience to be undergone. In a certain sense, prayer is indeed an experience but it is important to see that someone entering into prayer with the primary motive of gaining a valuable experience for himself or herself might well miss the experience, because he or she might not be surrendering to God, might still be trying to be in control of the situation in order to try to achieve something. Prayer is surrender to God, a letting go into the hands of the Other. The prime motive is service. We serve God in prayer. His glory and his Kingdom are paramount. What happens to us is his business, not ours. We hand over the fruits of prayer to him, not seeking anything for ourselves, content to let God control any experiences we may obtain out of the encounter with him. As we will see in a later chapter, the experience God sees fit to give us in prayer may be, for months, even years, the experience of boredom. At other times our experience may be consciously deep and richly fulfilling. What matters is not to be concerned about experience in prayer, but to draw the focus of attention away from ourselves so that it may

centre on God. 'In his will is our peace.' The paradox is that
we experience peace when we forget about aiming for it and
concern ourselves only with God's honour and glory. If we
remember that prayer is service of God, not cultivation of
self, we will avoid the mistake of approaching prayer as if it
were a 'thing'. With so much written about prayer (this
book included!) there is an ever present danger that we
approach prayer as if it were the goal itself of our exercise –
whereas, of course, God is the goal, and prayer only the
means towards him. It is not helpful, therefore, except as an
initial transitory position, to say that we love prayer or that
prayer does this or that to our lives. The truth is that we love
God in prayer or by prayer, for after all prayer is only the
medium of communication between us and God and it is
missing the point to linger too much on the means instead
of the end. In prayer our hearts should be engaged on God,
not on prayer. In the same way it is not prayer which has an
effect on people's lives, but strictly speaking God acting on
them in prayer. A helpful way to think of prayer is to see it as
a window through which we look at God. We all know that
to concentrate on the glass of a window is to miss the view
outside. There is even a way of standing before a window
and using it as a mirror in which to see our reflection. When
that is done, the view outside the window is completely
forgotten. George Herbert summed it up:

> A man may look on glass
> On it may stay his eye;
> Or if he pleaseth, through it pass,
> And then the heavens espy.

It is, therefore, my hope that after reading this book the reader will be led to think more about God than about prayer.

Let us conclude this chapter on receptivity to God with the reflection that unless we learn to receive we cannot really love. The heart of love is not just activity, the overwhelming desire to go to the other and be busy serving the beloved. It also consists in receiving love, allowing the beloved to serve oneself and effect changes in one's life. This second aspect of love, the receptive element, is often missed by those who are active in helping other people. Their lives are full of love; they are seldom still in their busy concern to help others. If asked they would say they knew about love; it was what their lives were 'all about'. But they would be lacking in one indispensable element of love: receiving and being changed. Active professional people sometimes never learn to do that. They are so busy changing other people's lives that their own lives remain unchanged, unentered. The lesson they must learn before they really love is the lesson that they should receive as well as give, be changed by others as well as try to change them. Unless I allow my beloved to change me, the relationship between us is not that of love. So it is with prayer. As our prayer becomes more simple so it becomes more receptive. We cease trying to master God in our lives and allow him to master us. The gift of contemplative prayer is God's way of taking charge of our lives and opening us up in readiness to receive his love and so be transformed.

4

Some Theological Considerations

The first three chapters of this book have been descriptive. I have tried to describe what people experience when they take prayer seriously. Even allowing for differences in temperament and training it is remarkable how similar the experience of prayer is among diverse people. It seems to be the universal experience that the Christian's approach to God simplifies as it matures, into a personal, intuitive and receptive meeting between the self and God with no intermediaries. The chapter which now follows is about theology. It is time to notice that the experience of simplification in prayer described above is in accordance with the theology of grace. It is in fact what you would expect to happen if the grace of God is allowed free reign in someone's life. The characteristics noted above are in fact the expected results of the life of grace and have Christian revelation behind them. They are not the marginal discoveries of a few unusual people but the rightful inheritance of every baptized person.

Simple prayer is *receptive*, as we saw in the last chapter. It is a response to a search by God for us, not a search which we ourselves initiate. God calls, we respond. The initiative is with him. That is what experience in prayer, as we begin to live the life of the moulded clay in the potter's hands. This is entirely true to theology, where we are taught that 'there can be no way from man to God unless there has been first set in the wilderness a way from God to man' (Donald McKinnon). This truth is the fundamental one of Revelation. Both Old and New Covenants were initiatives of God, unilateral decisions of God to choose to love mankind, addressed first of all to the Chosen People from the time of Abraham to John the Baptist, and then, through Jesus Christ's redeeming work, to the whole of the human race. The covenant of grace means that: God has taken the initiative and come to men and women in their state of alienation from him, offering them new life, through his Son. This basic truth was echoed by Jesus in his calling of his apostles: 'You have not chosen me; I have chosen you.' (Jn 15:16). It should therefore come as no surprise to experience in prayer this truth that theology teaches, that the Christian life is God's initiative, not ours; God is in charge, not we ourselves; God is the master potter and we the moulded clay. The growth of receptivity in prayer is a growth into truth, the fundamental truth of God's initiating grace.

Simple prayer is *intuitive*. It is not a process of discursive reasoning, but of the sort of simple knowledge which people have of each other when they become intimate. You cannot put into words how you know a friend intimately, but you just know that you know him and that he knows you, without much explanation as to how it works. So it is

with contemplative prayer. You know God and you know
that he knows you, in a simple, intuitive way, which needs
no long explanations and cannot be submitted to analysis.
It is intuitive by nature. There is a theological truth behind
this experience too. It is the truth, explained by theologians,
that by grace man is *elevated* beyond his natural capacities
and expectations to a kind of 'equality' with God. In this
totally given 'equality' men and women can be said to be
living the life of God (supernatural life) while still having a
human and perhaps sinful natural life. This new life of grace
enables baptized persons to commune with God as adopted
children of his family, that is, in a 'familiar' way. The work
of the Holy Spirit in baptized persons is precisely described
by St Paul in terms of familiar talking with God in prayer.
Redeemed people are able to talk to God because they have
the Holy Spirit in them.

> 'But when the time had fully come, God sent
> forth his Son, born of a woman, born under
> the law, to redeem those who were under the
> law, so that we might receive adoption as sons.
> And because you are sons, God has sent the
> Spirit of his Son into our hearts, crying, "Abba!
> Father!" '
>
> (Gal 4:4–6)

The intuitive prayer we have been discussing cannot be
better expressed than by the use of the term 'abba' ('Dad') in
our communion with God.

The above passage from the Epistle to the Galatians helps
us to remember that grace is not a 'thing', some sort of

spiritual 'stuff' or energy, which is given to baptized persons to help them live the Christian life. Grace is not a thing, but a Person, the presence of God's Spirit in our souls. This biblical truth is being re-emphasized today after centuries during which the popular estimate of grace became extremely reified. You prayed for, even earned, special graces which enabled you to achieve certain spiritual things. In popular preaching and devotion these graces were much to the fore. In the process the personal presence of God in our lives and the personal communion we have with him were forgotten in favour of the impersonal 'special grace' approach. A good example was the 'grace of a happy death.' We prayed for this. It was preached about. It was the reward promised to those who did the Nine First Fridays. It was the ultimately desirable thing, the crown of a lifetime's pursuit. But in the process of popularizing it, this special grace came to be seen in impersonal terms, a thing to be worked for, like a cup for winning a race. It was overlooked that the grace of a happy death is supremely personal, consisting simply in meeting God face to face and being accepted by him. What could be more personal than that? Graces, in other words, are best described as personal engagements between ourselves and God and not in such a way as to lead people to think of them as things. The best way to see grace is as the gift from God which enables us to converse with him, saying abba in our hearts. Grace is the ability given us by God to commune with him intimately.

Simple prayer is *personal*. Meditation tends to be impersonal: Rodin's *Thinker* turned in upon himself. Contemplative prayer is like *Jacob* wrestling with the angel, a real

meeting with God, person to person. The theology of grace
backs this experience up. The kernel of grace is the teaching
that in baptism we are adopted into God's family, are given
a new set of relationships within the Trinity. We can call
God our Father ('Abba'), because grace makes us his children, elevated beyond being mere creatures. We can call
Christ our Brother, because grace enables us to enter into
the mystery of the Incarnation, whereby the Son of God
became man and descended to become our equal, like us in
all things but sin. In fact, so much are we brothers and
sisters of Christ that we are given 'the mind of Christ',
become like-minded to him, as often occurs in a family.
Lastly we are given the Holy Spirit who dwells in our
inmost being and personally transforms us from within. By
grace we are elevated well beyond our station into the
family of God, into the heart of the Trinity. That is the
theological reason why a Christian's converse with God
tends from the beginning towards being a personal communion, direct and intimate. This means that those whose
prayer simplifies early on into a personal, intuitive process
are experiencing a normal and to be expected development.
This has to be said, because there is sometimes an erroneous
assumption that beginners in prayer must spend years at
vocal prayers and meditation and ought not to attempt a
contemplative approach as that would be to treat God too
familiarly. The other side of this assumption is that those
who do pray contemplatively are exceptional people, doing
something far beyond the vocation ordinary Christians.
Both aspects of the assumption contradict the theology of
grace. From the beginning grace makes us children of God,

members of his family. So from the beginning we are invited, undeservedly, to be familiar with him in prayer. It follows that those who do that are not exceptional souls, but are merely allowing their baptismal grace to develop in the normal way.

I do not want to give an impression of glibness in talking about familiarity with God in prayer. It does indeed happen that we become intimate with God in prayer, but in the process we do not lose the sense of God's greatness, his infinity. He remains GOD, the ineffable Creator who 'dwells in inaccessible light' and cannot be grasped by the human mind because he is too far above it. In other words, alongside the growth of familiarity with God in contemplative prayer there also grows a corresponding *awe* that this should ever be. The gap between creature and and Creator remains infinite and awesome. But by grace we are allowed to bridge it! God has stepped across it in his Son Jesus Christ (Incarnation), and we in the Spirit of Jesus are allowed to correspond back (Adoption as children of God). A supernatural elevation of our faculties has taken place and the wonder of contemplative prayer is that we can be familiar (Abba!) even with the infinite Creator. As we grow in intimacy with God we also grow in wonder. If prayer loses that wonder an element of truth has been lost, a wrong turning has been taken.

A good way to understand the theology of prayer is to reflect on the phrase used by St Paul, that by grace we are given the 'mind of Christ' (1 Cor 2:16). In his life and mission Jesus of Nazareth experienced certain key moments of closeness to God which have been described as 'abba

experiences.' The first was as a twelve-year-old boy in the
Temple at Jerusalem. His description to Mary and Joseph of
what he had been doing when they eventually caught up
with him was not in terms of Temple or Law, those two
Old Testament absolutes for the Jewish people. He simply
said that he had been in 'his Father's house.' Clearly the
adolescent boy had received a special experience of God as
his Father during those few days on his own away from his
parents. Eighteen years later Jesus inaugurated his public
life by receiving baptism from John and as he came out of
the water underwent an explicit 'abba experience.' The
Father's voice spoke to him and called him his 'beloved
Son.' This event sent him into the desert for forty days to
pray and ponder over its implications. At other times too in
the gospel we are given glimpses into Jesus' prayer life, both
in the ecstasy of transfiguration: 'This is my beloved Son;
listen to him' (Mark 9:7), and in the agony of Gethsemane:
'Abba, Father, all things are possible to thee; remove this cup
from me; Yet not what I will, but what thou wilt' (Mk
14:36). These explicit incidents give an insight into the
persisting implicit communion which Jesus maintained
with his Father, both in those nights in prayer on the
hillsides and in the busy days of work going about his
Father's business. We see that the whole of Jesus' life was a
prolonged 'abba experience.'

The mind of Christ, therefore, which we are given in
baptism is none other than the ability to commune with
God as Father in the same intimate way that Jesus did. In
other words grace is an entry into the simple communion of
contemplative prayer, not stopping short out of false humil-

ity at the stage when we treat God as a stranger, but allowing the intimacy of friendship to blossom beyond conceivable limits. The fact that the experience is in no way earned but is sheer gift only increases the wonder. It does not take away from the fact.

Theologically speaking the exercise of prayer is an exercise of the virtues of faith, hope and charity. We love god in prayer (charity) but in this life it is tempered by faith and trust. We do not see God or in any way pass beyond the veil of faith. All use of words like 'see' to describe prayer is metaphorical. In practice prayer is often a dark, unseeing experience, calling upon all our powers of hanging on in fidelity. We see very little, and what we do see are the effects of God in this world and in our souls, not God himself. To say this is compatible with saying that in prayer we have the mind of Christ, because as described in the gospels Jesus had to exercise much faith and frequently walked in darkness, for instance in Gethsemane. A good description of the prayer of Jesus is given in the Epistle to the Hebrews:

> 'In the days of his flesh, Jesus offered up prayers
> and supplications, with loud cries and tears, to
> him who was able to save him from death, and
> he was heard for his godly fear. Although he was
> a Son, he learnt obedience through what he
> suffered.'
>
> (5:7–8)

Theology tells us that when we pray this same Christ prays in us. Now he is in glory sitting at the right hand of the

Father, but in us, members of his Body, he continues to pray the prayer of faith which in history he prayed on the hillsides of Galilee and in Jerusalem from the cross itself. In Christ we pray with the intimacy which that 'being in Christ' gives us, but always in faith and trust, not yet face to face.

Aids

5

The Gift Of Time

In the next chapter we will discuss techniques of prayer, but more important than any technique to introduce us to the life of prayer is the giving of time to it. By giving time to prayer we ensure that we actually set out upon the adventure of praying. It is unfortunately all too easy to remain theoretical in prayer, and one of the ways we do that is by reading and discussing all the various techniques for praying: Christian, non-Christian, traditional, up-to-date, abstracting from the body, using the body, following the schools of the past, Spanish, French, medieval English, and so on. For beginners this is a mistake, since it can be a substitute for actually getting down to the business of praying. Theoretical discussion about prayer techniques before the decision to pray is as if we lay in bed in the morning pondering the best way to get up (left leg first? right leg first?) and successfully postponed the moment for doing it. The only way to get out of bed in the morning is to do it! The only way to pray is to pray – and later examine the ways and means of it. The time for discussion of techniques and schools of prayer is after, not before, we are regularly giving time to it.

Another reason for giving time to prayer before too much examination of theory is that in prayer, as we have seen,

God is the chief actor and we the acted upon. If we make ourselves too busy scrutinising the ways of prayer at the outset, we run the risk of being too active and so never learning to be passive in prayer, even as we are reading about its necessity. To be truly receptive we have to launch upon a generous allocation of time to prayer without knowing much about what will happen in that time. An act of faith that God will look after us in prayer is needed, not a calculated mastery of the subject to prevent ourselves feeling lost. As we saw in chapter 3, those who try to master the art of prayer do not get very far because they do not allow God to be the master.

The giving of time to someone is the gift of self. We give time, ungrudgingly, to people who mean a lot to us because we want to give ourselves to them. On the other hand we do not give time to people who mean little to us or who bore us. As the saying goes, we have no time for them. We have no time for them because we do not feel inclined to share much of ourselves with them. Often with people who do not mean much to us we decide to give something less than the whole of ourselves, so we give money or advice. Both forms of giving effectively short cut the process of engagement and allow us to be disengaged. It is easier to give money to a poor man at the door than to have him into your house and share a cup of tea with him. By giving him money you quickly get rid of him. If he came into your house, he might speak about himself, enter into your life and be a burden upon you. In the same way, as all counsellors know, to give advice rather than listen is a most effective way of bringing an interview to an end before too much time is wasted. As with friends, so with God. The measure of how much we want to give our whole selves to God in prayer is the measure of how much time we are prepared to give to it. As Abbot Chapman said, 'the less you pray, the worse it goes.' Conversely, other things being equal, the more you pray, the better it goes.

When in the 1960s the concept of prayer was under attack and many people considered it out of date and unsuitable for man 'come of age,' various attempts were made to justify it. These often consisted in demonstrating how valuable time spent in prayer was for the individual. It was a time for recouping energies, for encountering self at a deeper level than before, for reviewing life in the presence of the Eternal. The common feature of these justifications was the attempt to prove how *valuable* time spent in prayer was. While not denying what was then argued in favour of prayer, I would put forward another argument: that prayer is a 'waste of time.' In terms of time we need not set out to get anything out of it. There is, after all, still an element of self-seeking in seeing prayer as valuable for me; but to see prayer as a waste of time opens up to us the giving element in prayer. We do not pray in order to gain something for ourselves. We pray in order to give something to God. It is a sacrifice. That is the language of love. The language of lovers is waste, especially the wasting of time in each other's company. Nobody likes to waste time with someone who is not particularly important to him or her; but we all run to waste time with our friends and beloveds. That, I suggest, is how we grow in prayer: by the apparently foolhardy decision to sacrifice generous periods of our personal time with no eye on what we stand to gain from it, but simply out of love for God our Father to whom we are entrusting our lives. In a busy life that proves to be a considerable sacrifice and act of faith. A story from the gospel illustrates the generosity which Jesus evoked in his followers: 'Mary took a pound of costly ointment of pure nard, and anointed the feet of Jesus and wiped his feet with her hair; and the house was filled with the fragrance of the ointment' (Jn 12:3). It was a gesture of complete waste, perhaps a lifetime's savings spent in one act of love: no hope for any gain; no husbanding of resources to be better spent at a later date; just a grand gesture of love for the person of Jesus, completed in a few minutes. We know that Judas criticized the action in terms which make much sense in contemporary times: 'Why was this ointment not sold for three hundred denarii and given to the poor?' If that had been done we should never have heard of Mary's action, and the gospel would have been robbed of one of its most telling narratives. The spirit of the gospel is in Mary's wasteful act of love and not in Judas' prudent strategy. We need to remember that spirit of Mary when we pray, because there is little of common sense or prudence in the adventure of prayer. It is an exercise of love, and love has this disconcerting element of crazy waste in it.

In practice we are asked to show generosity in prayer less in grand gestures than by the humdrum virtue of fidelity, hanging on when there are no visible results to be seen. I hope the reader has not been misled by previous passages about intimacy with God in the silent communion of love into thinking that the actual exercise of prayer is always noticeably rewarding. This is far from the case. The practice of contemplative prayer is frequently dull, even boring. This is because men and women are not naturally tuned in to silent communion with the Invisible. At one level it is always unrewarding. This is the level in us which responds to sense stimuli, a level which is spectacularly titillated in our modern consumer society to a degree unknown in the past. At this level prayer is bound to be unattractive. Fortunately it is neither that only level we live on, nor the one at which we are most ourselves. This latter level, the spiritual in man, is where our true selves exist and where our most authentic actions take place. It is, of course, the level at which we engage God and are engaged by him in prayer. It is, therefore, essential when we begin to pray for any length of time to face the problem of the boredom which will come to us. We must not be surprised to be bored in prayer. Still less should we feel guilty, for the reason given above. Our superficial self is rebelling at the lack of stimuli presented to it, but this is no cause for dismay or guilt, merely for acceptance. On the other hand the phenomenon of boredom should not be greeted so casually that we learn nothing from it. We must tackle it calmly but strongly with fidelity, a resolute decision to stay in relationship with God in prayer, and fix our hearts firmly on him.

The reward for this fidelity will be the discovery that dryness in prayer is not a dead end with nothing beyond it, but a threshold. Sooner or later the aridity gives way to the realization that we can commune with God very happily at the deeper level. The exercise of fidelity has activated powers within us to share with God in our deeper selves, powers which up to then were dormant and unknown to us, and which have only come to life because brought into action by the inactivity on the surface and the need to do something about it. Inactivity on the surface has led us to discover rich action and exchange at a deeper level.

How much time should we give to prayer? There can be no mathematical answer valid for every reader. Because we are all so different both in temperament and in circumstances, this is not a matter for public discussion but should be taken up personally with a spiritual guide. The fact that we bother to take the matter up with someone can itself be a sign that we are serious about prayer. With regard to a general principle concerning time spent in prayer, anything less than half an hour at a time tends to be too short for deep engagement. We cannot get far in a friendship if we only spend short fifteen minute periods with our friend. At least half an hour is essential for the relationship to deepen. It is the same with God in prayer.

Some people find it helpful to organize their prayer life on a weekly rather than a daily basis and think in terms of a half-hour period once a week for prayer and spiritual reading, say on a Saturday. This corresponds with the urban life cycle. Country life organizes itself round the twenty-four hour cycle. There are things to be done every morning and evening, like milking the cows. City life, however, tends to go in a seven day cycle with weekly rather than daily jobs to be done, like giving the house a thorough cleaning, or filling up the store cupboard at the supermarket. That being so, it may be more meaningful to think of giving time for prolonged prayer on a once a week basis, putting aside a deliberately generous amount of time per week for personal prayer, as one would a visit to one's grandmother or family friend. If, as we said above, we measure the value of our friends by the amount of time we are prepared to waste with them, a review of our weekly life should ensure that we allocate plenty of time for communing with God in prayer.

It goes without saying that we have to exercise self-discipline in setting aside time for prayer. That surface part of ourselves which needs attractive stimuli must not be allowed to make unaided decisions about prayer. The deeper part where we commune with God in prayer must be allowed to control our superficial selves. In particular we must know ourselves well enough not to be misled by various escape formulae which we use in order to deceive ourselves. A favourite one is 'I've no time to …' We use the phrase to avoid duties which are uncongenial. It is frequently used to avoid a serious engagement with prayer. We say, 'I would like to pray, but I've no time to.' At this point we should pause and ask ourselves if this be true. Have we no time for prayer, or is it really that we have no inclination? Facing this subterfuge honestly and then taking appropriate action is a first step in entering into the life of prayer deeply and seriously. A friend who had to go to the hospital to tune into a kidney machine three times a week, on Mondays, Wednesdays and Fridays, for two hours each time, told me that it was remarkable how readily he found time in a busy life for this which he knew to be essential. He never found himself saying he had no time for it. He proved to himself the truth that we always have time for things and persons we know to be important. The beginning of prayer life is the realization that God *is* important and worth giving time to!

A second formula we sometimes use in order to postpone a serious engagement with prayer is to say that rather than set aside specific time for meeting God in prayer, we are going to pray all the time during our work and recreation, for God is present everywhere and all the time, and so can be reached that way. There is a golden truth in this statement. Perhaps there are some people who can avail themselves of the fact and reach God from the start in his continuing presence in this world. Experience, however, shows that most men and women need to practise specific prayer assiduously before they can hope to retain an awareness of God constantly in their daily lives. The truth is that we only learn to pray all the time everywhere after we have resolutely set about praying some of the time somewhere. Those who do manage to pray constantly in every moment are also the ones who long to be able to find specific periods for prayer undisturbed by any other occupation. Usually they succeed in this quest and so make nonsense of the beginners' avoidance of specific prayer time in favour of prayerful activity.

In Christianity the good is sometimes the enemy of the best. This proves to be true in the matter of finding time for prayer. In order to find time to pray we have not only to give up the bad things in our life which are sinful, but also numerous good things. The things with which we occupy our leisure moments like reading, watching television, conversation with friends, sleep, are entirely good and not to be condemned. Nevertheless relative to prayer they are not the best; so the person who sets out to go deep in prayer sometimes has to sacrifice them in order to find the space and time to pray. It seems absurd to be avoiding such worthwhile occupations as sleep or reading, but those who have made the sacrifice in order to pray in a prolonged way are certain that the sacrifice was effective. They discern in the realm of their relationship to God what all lovers instinctively know: that any sacrifice is worth making to be with the beloved.

6

Spiritual Reading

An essential point of departure for prayer is reading. Because prayer is an exercise of our minds as well as our hearts, we should be constantly feeding our minds with thoughts about God and the work of salvation performed by Jesus Christ and the Holy Spirit. Unless we fill our minds with reflection about these supernatural realities we will have no body of thought with which to start our prayer. Surrounded as we are with glittering superficialities presented to us by the media and by our day to day meetings with fellow human beings, we need positively to decide to think about God if we are to preserve a true sense of Reality in our lives. The most real in this world is the most invisible; but because invisible the most easily forgotten. Reading about these invisible realities of our Faith corrects the tendency for our hold on the invisible to lessen. It feeds our minds with the Truth. Then it warms our hearts towards the Truth, and we begin to pray. The monks of old knew this and prescribed that as much time each day should be spent in spiritual reading ('lectio divina') as in prayer.

What to read? The answer is any book that helps us at the present time. There is no virtue in persevering with a book that is not helping us to pray, even if it is soundly recom-

mended and has helped others. A sensible rule is to persevere only with the books which provide nourishment here
and now. Later on, as we develop and change, we may find
ourselves growing to like a book which before had no
appeal to us. Conversely we often find that books which
used to be favourites lose their appeal, sometimes to such an
extent that we wonder how we ever found them helpful. All
this means is that, as we grow, we change our tastes in
spiritual books as much as we change our tastes in secular
reading. The unpredictability of our tastes is an extra excite-
ment in the life of prayer. As individuals we are children of
the age we live in. One reason for change in personal tastes
in spirituality is that whole generations change as well as
persons. As the generations grow out of one kind of spiritual reading into another, so individuals do the same. Every
religious house has shelves in its library containing spiritual
books which were favourites and best sellers fifty years ago
and which are now unreadable and unread. They gather
dust as witnesses to the changing tastes of mankind. In the
same way the popular books of this generation will in their
turn become unreadable and unread. The few exceptions to
this are the classics of Christian literature which somehow
survive the test of time.

There is one book, or collection of books, which never
dates: the Bible. The Bible has proved relevant to every
generation of Christians. When those dusty 19th century
spiritual books were popular the Bible was still central, as it
is now when a wholly different type of spiritual book is
being read. This is because the Old and New Testaments are
the prime sources of God's intentions towards mankind.

They are in a different category from any other Christian books, being the sources of revelation which other books comment upon. The message of the Bible is, of course, relevant to every age, simply because God is relevant to every age; but the language and culture of the Bible is not. The various books it contains each bring with them their own out of date culture, which has to be interpreted by each generation of Christians who read the Scriptures. The out-of-date-ness of the Bible makes for hard work by the scholars, but it also makes for a certain stability. One can turn to the Bible knowing that one is not subscribing to a passing theological or spiritual fashion. The Bible has a reassuring everlastingness which allows it to speak with equal effect to every age. It never gathers dust on the shelves or is relegated to history. It is, after all, the Word of God.

There are two ways of reading the Bible. The first is to approach it scientifically and examine it from the point of view of its human authors: who they were, what they intended to say, what was their background, what, there-fore, are the hidden references which would mean much to their original audiences but have to be researched by us if we are to reveal anything. From this follows some theologi-cal reflection. For instance in St Luke's account of the Transfiguration it is said that Jesus discussed with Moses and Elijah the 'Exodus' he was to accomplish in Jerusalem. This is a reference which will mean a lot to the reader who knows the significance of the Exodus in Jewish faith and in Christian theology. Without such rudimentary scriptural knowledge, however, the reference will be lost, and a richer meaning of the Transfiguration will remain undetected by the reader. One will have missed a fruitful reflection on the event of the Transfiguration which was in the author's mind when he wrote it down. This is one of many examples of how an understanding of the Old Testament greatly enriches our reading of the New.

I am not suggesting that every Christian needs to be a scholar, but I think that all of us should be aware of the findings of the scholars about each book of the Bible. Nowadays this background knowledge is readily available in the introductions and footnotes to our Bibles. To neglect to become acquainted with these is to close the door on many riches lying within the Old and New Testaments. If, on the other hand, we take reading our Bibles seriously enough to absorb this background knowledge of God's revelation, our prayer lives will be great helped. A healthy feature of the post-Vatican II Church is the growth of Bible study groups and circles in ordinary parish life. These are excellent aids to prayer for the participants.

Knowing the scientific background to the books of the Bible is, however, only a preliminary to prayer. Prayer begins when we start to read our Bible listening primarily no longer to the historical human authors, but to God, the supreme Author. Prayer begins when we listen to what God is saying to us at the present moment through our reading of a passage. 'One must read the Bible as a young man reads a letter from his beloved. It is written for me,' declared Kierkegaard. When this happens, our scientific knowledge of the passage recedes into the background and gives way to a direct, prayerful listening to the message from God. We are listening directly to God through the inspired page before us. The critical ear has given way to the receptive ear. We slowly read, ponder, and pray the passage, in no hurry to finish it, ready to pause and listen for a long time, should we feel inclined no to move on. Of course the preliminary reading has been useful in its time, but now it is left behind as we give full rein to our desire to be with God, listening to his will for us, not critically but in obedience.

The essence of this sort of reading is to read slowly and openly. We have to read slowly, because quick reading detects only the surface meaning of any passage; deeper meanings take time to surface in our minds. When I get a letter from someone who means much to me, I open and read it eagerly, but then I do not throw it away. I keep it, and later in the day will read it again. I repeat this lovingly for days on end. Each time I read the letter, I see more meaning in it, because I have been analysing it for hidden information: Why did she say that? Why did she not answer that question I put to her? Why did she end in that way? The more I read the letter, the more I see in it. It becomes less a question of reading and more a question of meditative pondering, even a loving communion with the absent correspondent. This loving process is what the monastic tradition calls 'lectio divina.' It is both slow, as described above, and open, because one reads not for the sake of taking information into oneself but in order to go outward to one's absent friend in silent communion. Von Hügel likened this meditative spiritual reading to 'dissolving a lozenge on the tongue.' All spiritual books need to be read in this way, but especially the Bible, which is God's Word. I conclude this chapter on spiritual reading with a desription which comes in a book by W.W.E. Orchard *From Faith to Faith*. He describes his old grandfather, a simple labouring man, a nonconformist in the English tradition.

> 'When he came home from work, after his meal, he shaved, dressed himself more carefully, and then settled down to the Bible, set under the lamp on the table before him. When the Book had been opened at the proper place, his spectacles had to be carefully polished, to the accompaniment of anticipatory sighs over the treasures he was about to explore. The spectacles being then as carefully adjusted, a verse was slowly read, half aloud to himself. Deeper sighs then followed, perhaps accompanied by the exclamation, 'This Blessed Book!' Further reflections would bring forth joyful tears, which meant that the spectacles had to be wiped again; and so on, but always with the same deliberation.
>
> A visiting minister used to tell how, coming in upon him one evening during these pious exercises (for he was slightly deaf, which made it possible for him sometimes to be observed unknown) he enquired what was giving him such evident joy, and was told that it was the 8th of Romans: 'I have been on it all the week,' he explained.
>
> 'And how far have you got?'

'The 5th verse' was the reply; and this was Thursday night!' This is spiritual reading of the deepest kind, reading which has passed from meditation to contemplation under the influence of the inspired Word of God.

7

Some Methods

Reading is indispensable for growth in the life of prayer. What about methods and techniques? In one sense they are not necessary, since all we need is to have the will to pray and to leave the rest to God. Nevertheless it is helpful and saves unnecessary floundering to have some simple methods to enable us to begin to pray and, after that, to grow. Techniques in prayer must never be allowed to become the central issue, but provided they are kept as aids to communion with God and do not become the focus of attention, they are valuable. This chapter is about simple methods for beginners in contemplation.

The Our Father

It takes about fifteen seconds to say the Lord's Prayer at speaking pace. A good introduction to simple and silent prayer is to make it take fifteen minutes. When you do this you commit yourself to plenty of silent periods between each phrase of the prayer, in order to make prayer last the whole fifteen minutes. Thus: 'Our Father' – pause – 'who art in heaven' – pause ... At first the pauses tend to be awkward and empty, but with practice they become charged with meaning, meaning given to each by the phrase which has preceded it. Soon, with perseverance (and, of course, the grace of God), the periods of silence between the phrases begin to mean more than the phrases themselves; they are filled with communion with God, silent, and intensely personal, reaching down into our hearts further than words can go. Sometimes it is possible merely to say 'Our Father' (Abba!) and let that one phrase suffice for the whole period of prayer. This comes with perseverance, not always quickly. However, we must not make a judgment about how 'advanced' we are in prayer by the amount of time we can spend in silence without need for a new phrase. Sometimes a day when silence comes quickly and easily is followed by a day when it is impossible, and we have to repeat formulas over and over again to enable us to pray at all. What matters is that we persevere, and the formula of the Lord's own prayer is an excellent one with which to stay. We may be certain that it will lead us towards silent contemplation. It is worth reading the passage in the Sermon on the Mount where Jesus teaches his disciples to pray the Our Father (Mt 6:5–15). Notice Jesus' admonition not to 'heap up empty phrases as the Gentiles do.' For Jesus, clearly, much speaking in prayer was to be avoided. Those nights spent on the hillsides with his Father were surely spent in silent communion.

The Jesus Prayer

Jesus gave another instruction on prayer, this time in St Luke's Gospel, taking the form of a parable:

'Two men went up into the temple to pray,
one a Pharisee and the other a tax collector.
The Pharisee stood and prayed thus with
himself, "God, I thank thee that I am not like
other men, extortioners, unjust, adulterers, or
even like this tax collector. I fast twice a week,
I give tithes of all that I get." But the tax
collector, standing far off, would not lift up
his eyes to heaven, but beat his breast, saying,
"God, be merciful to me a sinner!" I tell you,
this man went down to his house justified
rather than the other; for everyone who exalts
himself will be humbled, but he who humbles
himself will be exalted.'

(Luke 18:9–14)

This parable contains one of the central messages of the
gospel, well captured in Mauriac's phrase 'the sinner is at the
heart of Christendom.' We are all sinners and fall short of
perfection. The important difference is not in the degree of
wickedness between one sinner and another but in the
degree of recognition of our sinfulness. In the parable the
tax collector was closer to God because he recognized his
need for God's merciful forgiveness more than did the
Pharisee. Unlike the Pharisee he knew that he needed God
and needed to pray. Paradoxically we come closer to God
the more we recognize our sins and therefore think we are
farther away from him. This crucial paradox separates 'the
Unjust' who are dear to God from 'the Just' whom Jesus
castigated.

Out of this teaching of Jesus on true humility has come a classical prayer, the Jesus Prayer. It is a simple formula, based on the prayer of the tax collector: '*Jesus, Son of God, have mercy on me, a sinner.*' To pray the Jesus Prayer one takes the four phrases of the formula and repeats them slowly and rhythmically as many times as one wants to. It is good to set up a rhythm in repeating the phrases. Some people do this by associating the phrases with their breathing: Jesus (IN): Son of God (OUT): have mercy on me (IN): a sinner (OUT). This enables the whole of the person to be praying, not just the mind or voice. In this way you make the whole of your being express the gospel and build up a rhythm which passes beyond mere vocalization to existence itself. The final outcome is to shorten the formula to the single word 'Jesus' which then stands for the complete formula and becomes the prayer of your whole self. When we remember that 'Jesus' means 'the Lord is salvation' we see that shortening the prayer to its first word sums up the whole phrase in an admirable way. Generations of Christians, especially in the East, have made the Jesus Prayer the chief expression of their Christianity. History has made it almost as important as the Lord's Prayer itself. In some moods, moods of failure or depression, I have found the Jesus Prayer the only possible way of making contact with God. Other ways of praying have seemed too demanding or too 'perfect'. In my failure I have welcomed the publican's prayer for mercy with thankfulness, because it means that even though I have alienated myself from God by sin, I can still approach him in prayer by penitence and this cry for mercy.

Short Phrases

We have already seen that there is a tendency for formulas in prayer to shorten into one or two words only. The Our Father becomes simply 'Abba Father,' the Jesus Prayer becomes the one word 'Jesus.' This tendency increases as we grow into contemplative prayer and feel at ease with silent communion. It is natural to want to let a few heavily significant words stand duty for whole phrases, because love expresses itself better in few words and silence than in many sentences. Consequently a good method in prayer is to choose a few favourite expressions and slowly repeat them to God. Abba Father! You are Lord! King of Glory! I love you! I thank you! Come Holy Spirit! Everyone finds his or her own best expression for the moment. Some stay with one word ('mantra') for their whole life; others vary their phrases according to the moods and needs of the present. Notice that each of these phrases is addressed to God; it is not addressed to oneself about God. 'You are Lord,' for instance, not 'He is Lord.' By doing this, we ensure that our prayer remains outward going, an engagement with the other, not a piece of meditation with oneself. Once again we align ourselves with Jacob wrestling with the Angel, not with the solitary Thinker.

The Psalms

Someone who has been led into the way of the use of formula prayers in a contemplative fashion will find the psalms a rich treasure for prayer. They can be prayed in many ways. Their first use is their public recitation or singing in the offices of the Church. They can also be prayer privately. One can recite a psalm from beginning to end, following its 'argument' and making that one's own. One can also take the verses of a psalm slowly and allow oneself to dwell on any phrase that strikes, staying with that phrase and letting it express one's approach to God for a whole day. There is no need to finish the whole psalm. Any verse can be selected and stayed with as long as one chooses. Here are four such precious phrases. But there are countless others.

> 'My soul, give thanks to the Lord.
> all my being, bless his holy name.'

> 'Guide my heart to fear your name.'
> 'O God, we ponder your love
> within your temple.'

> 'You are my hiding place, O Lord;
> you save me from distress.'

We seldom open the Psalter without coming upon a word or phrase that seems just right for our particular needs. In the hundred and fifty psalms every mood and aspiration of the human spirit is to be found, ranging from gloomy despair to exultant joy, or from respectful obedience towards God to anger against him for abandoning the psalmist in the face of enemies. Consequently through the ages the psalms have proved a never-ending source of inspiration to every kind of Christian. Among those who used them was Jesus Christ. They must have played a large part in his spiritual formation. This alone should make us want to use them in our spiritual lives.

The gradual psalms (nos 119–135), which were sung by pilgrims going up to Jerusalem are mostly short, and contain beautiful pictures of the Israelites at prayer. Psalm 122 has this picture:

> 'Like the eyes of a servant
> on the hands of her mistress
> so our eyes are on the Lord our God
> till he shows us his mercy.'

This well describes the attitude of the soul at prayer: content to wait patiently, as it were behind the throne, watching for a sign from the mistress. 'Take this plate away,' 'Open the window,' ready to obey with promptitude. Even if no sign comes, the servant remains waiting, fulfilling her duty by serving, whether she is actively doing something or not. The psalm underlines the fact that prayer is primarily a service performed by attentive duty and can be perfectly fulfilled even if nothing happens. Experience is secondary to the whole exercise, which is adequately performed with or without the sensation of personal fulfillment and satisfaction.

The Body

It is a mistake to ignore the body in prayer. It is an even greater mistake to think the body is a hindrance to prayer on the grounds that it is material, not spiritual. My body is me. It is the external sign of my soul. What my body performs are my actions. What I receive with my soul I receive through my bodily senses: sight, touch, taste, hearing, smell. It is therefore important to let the body become involved in prayer. If the body is not allowed to cooperate in prayer it will prove a hindrance to prayer by staging a revolt of boredom, or noisy distractions. The Catholic instinct recognizes this and has always enlisted the cooperation of the body in prayer by genuflections, bows, signs of the cross, appeals to the ears, eyes and even the sense of smell in incense.

The quiet simple prayer which we have been concerned with in this book has a part for the body to play. We can train the body to be still, quiet, attentive, and so exercise a calming influence on the mind in prayer. In fact the shortest way to stilling the mind is by being still first in the body. A disciplined, tranquil body is a pre-requisite for a disciplined, tranquil heart and mind. The disciplined attention of our body is for many of us not easily achieved, but it can be arrived at with practice. We can kneel or stand in prayer if we like, but the best position is to sit. Sitting in prayer should be with a straight back, preferably not leaning against anything, but allowing the spine to be upright, taking the thrust of one's weight vertically downwards into the ground. The sort of easy lounge chair which most of us sit in is particularly bad for prayer. To sit on an upright, hard chair, or on the ground is best. Then one can let go gently, allowing the ground to receive one's weight through one's buttocks, and letting the tranquility which slowly spreads through one's body to pass into the soul as well. For people who have been rushing about motorcars, elevators, sidewalks, corridors, the first exercise in prayer could be just to sit and allow the body to become still, paying full attention to the relaxing of one's muscles, before even considering the presence of God. We have to be present to our own selves, first body, then mind, before attempting to be present to God. Be still and know that I am here – then, be still and know that God is here.

A special significance attaches to one of our bodily functions: breathing. It is the most central of all those functions being the one associated with life itself. It is the vital function. While we breathe we live. When breath is squeezed out, we cease to exist. Naturally, then, breathing has been taken seriously by religious people, because it is the corporal point at which we meet the spiritual Creator God. Breathing is the contact point between God and me. To become conscious of my breathing and to do it 'with meaning,' religiously, is to become conscious of God creating me, breathing his Spirit into me. The Bible sees the Spirit (or Breath) of God as present and operating in the two most important events of our life: at Creation and at Redemption. Both of them are continuous, not instantaneous. God sends his Spirit into us to create us out of nothing at every moment, and to recreate us in the new life of grace, equally continuously. A good way of praying is simply to make oneself conscious of one's breathing and to *feel* God's creative Spirit being infused into one, natural and supernatural life being inflated into one simultaneously. Most of the time we breathe completely unconsciously and automatically. In prayer we can become conscious and voluntary with regard to our breathing. This is best done by deliberately slowing one's breathing down, making it more solemn and important. It *is* important. It concerns our life. As we breathe in it is the Spirit of God being infused into us. This is followed by our breathing out, which expresses our partnership with the Holy Spirit in the praise of prayer and the zeal of good works. As we breathe in we receive; as we breathe out we cooperate.

This breathing prayer is a beautifully simple way of praying. It requires no apparatus, not even a book or a picture. The apparatus is oneself, doing what one has to do, anyway, all the time: simply breathing. But breathing prayerfully, with meaning, beginning to take the miracle of one's creation and the wonder of the new life of grace no longer for granted, but with grateful attention. This simple prayer of breathing, to which words can be attached or not (as the Jesus Prayer), can almost be called the prayer of Good News, for it enables us to celebrate the good news of the gospel, existentially, by participating voluntarily in God's gift of life and grace. We need look no further for proof of God's grace. It is here present in our bodies with every breath we breathe. The value of this prayer lies also in its lack of requirement of external apparatus or place. Wherever we are we have to breathe. We can, then, start to pray here and now, as we breathe, and need look no further for a special time or place. That time and place for prayer is now and here, as we stand in line in the shop, or sit in a car waiting for the traffic lights to change: 'Quick now, here, now, always – a condition of complete simplicity costing not less than everything.' In a few words the poet has summed up the magic of the continual presence of God and our personal surrender to him.

Growth in Gospel Value

8

Faith, Not Works

The reader who has got this far in the book may well ask how Christian it is to be concerned with prayer, prayer methods, spiritual reading, in a world where the majority of our fellow human beings are living subhuman lives either because they are exploited by the rich and powerful or simply because they have not got enough to eat. How Christian is it to be cultivating the art of prayer in the leisure moments of a privileged life instead of helping the underprivileged to gain freedom? Has, in fact, the subject of this book anything to do with the gospel of Jesus Christ in the world today? Is it not, rather, the drawing room pursuit of the relatively idle middle classes of the affluent western world? Facing these questions honestly compels us to examine the relationship between the Christian quality of our prayer and that of the remainder of our lives. If they are not closely connected, then indeed our prayer is not Christian, nor are our lives. This chapter examines the relationship between prayer and the rest of our lives.

The test of the quality of one's prayer is the quality of one's life. It is tempting to make the test of prayer how one feels during prayer. We do this automatically. Prayer has been smooth and easy; there have been few distractions; we have felt close to God. So we say that our prayer is good and that we have no problems with it. On another day, however, it has gone badly, dreadfully patchy and interrupted with distractions; we have not the presence of God at all. We conclude from this that there is something wrong with our prayer. In both these cases we are making the mistake of judging our prayer by our feelings during it. To do that is to make prayer an end in itself, something we do apart from everything else, unconnected with the rest of our life. That is, of course, not the case. Prayer is the articulated expression of our whole lives. We take the whole of our living, in prayer and outside prayer, and present it to God as an offering subject to his judgment. Prayer is nothing more than the explicit articulation of our lives offered to God. It is necessarily connected with how we are conducting our lives as children of God. Prayer, therefore, is intimately connected with what we do about the exploited poor of our world, and how we live the gospel in our lives. To put it bluntly, if we are not concerned about our neighbour in this world, then it is no use praying, since our prayer will be no good, simply self-indulgence, not Christian sacrifice.

If we accept the close connection between prayer and living, we will be able to understand that our conduct outside prayer is the best test of the quality of prayer. If our lives are found to be honest, truthful, caring of others, pure – or at least are a constant attempt to be so in spite of failures, then we may be sure that our prayer is good. Our lives are an attempt to please God, so our prayer is sincere, even if we felt it was no good. How we felt at prayer is not the point. The point is whether we tried to please God with our living of which prayer is simply an expression. If our lives were to be selfish and we were to give up the attempt to do God's will, but we still devoted time to prayer, that would be a sign that our prayer was insincere and hypocritical, even though it might be full of raptures. God could justly say to us, 'This people honours me with its lips but its heart is far from me.' In other words, the connection between prayer and the life which is lived on either side of it is intimate. The quality of my life will determine the quality of my prayer, and the quality of my prayer will have an effect on the life that follows it. Notice that in judging this quality the question of feelings does not enter. God's judgment on us is independent of whether we feel close to him or not. He judges us by our deeds and intentions, not by our feelings. Our prayer is good when our hearts are fixed on God, even if it is filled with boring aridity or passionate turmoil.

The more we pray the more the distinction between prayer and conduct becomes blurred. When we start we are conscious of two separate kinds of Christian action. One kind is conduct, the attempt to live our life as Christians according to the standards of Jesus Christ. The other kind is prayer, the attempt to communicate with God. We see them as two distinct things linked together. At this stage the link consists in directing our prayer towards making our conduct more Christian. We pray to become better people, to be more virtuous. With time, however, the separation in our minds between prayer and conduct begins to disappear; we see both kinds of response as action towards God to please him. We see the underlying unity of the whole of our life and recognize that our life is lived in the direction of God, and that both prayer and good acts are fundamentally expressions of our love of God; both are 'statements' to God. When this happens, it is beginning to be true that our whole life is prayer, that 'laborare est orare,' to work is to pray. Notice, however, that what is happening is that our conduct is becoming more akin to prayer; we are making what we do a more or less conscious attempt to relate to God.

Another way of describing this growing unification of our lives is to say that we become less preoccupied with morality (correct conduct, works), and more concerned with relating closely to God (faith, prayer). This was well put by William Temple in his aphorism about Christianity, that 'the right relation between prayer and conduct is not that conduct is supremely important and prayer helps it, but that prayer is supremely important and conduct is its test.' In Christianity, prayer, the attempt to relate our lives personally to God, is supremely important. The New Testament is not a moralistic document, full of prescriptions on how to live. It is a series of books, gospels and epistles, which declare that we are already living a new life, that we are closely related to God by grace, and that consequently our conduct will be changed for the better. The Christianity of the New Testament is not perfectionist, but relational. The new Christians are told about the unbelievably good news of their redemption in Christ, their being made children of God, able to call him Abba. The conduct expected of them is indeed outlined, but it is not made central to the message. The central message concerns the new relationship of being adopted children of God. Relationship to God (in faith, trust, love) was central for the early Christian converts, as it had demonstrably been in Jesus' life. You see this emphasis also in St Paul's epistles. St Paul's letters contain many exhortations to avoid sin and pursue virtue, coupled with lists of good works and bad work, but these always came at the end of his epistles and are presented as the result of the Christian being 'in Christ.' Virtue for St Paul is not an achievement to be aimed at so much as an inevitable fruit of the life of grace, described either as being in Christ (Ephesians, Colossians) or as salvation through faith, not works (Romans, Galatians). Prayer is supremely important and conduct is its fruit and test.

We are now in a position to answer the question posed at the beginning of this chapter. Is the cultivation of prayer at all Christian in a world which calls out for action to help our starving and exploited neighbour? It is Christian, we reply, because true prayer will be reflected in our actions, and the person who prays will be led to work for the Kingdom of God in this world, to hunger and thirst for God's justice. It is the experience of those who pray that they meet the living God, and are then turned round and sent back into the world of men and women to do his work. True prayer is not an escape from living but a dangerous advance into areas of living which were hitherto not suspected or experienced. The lives of the great mystics manifested this. People like Bernard of Clairvaux, Teresa of Avila, John of the Cross, who wrote unforgettably about prayer and cultivated it with dedication, were given lives of hectic activity in God's cause as a result of their prayer. The fact is they were not cultivating prayer, but cultivating God's will, and that is why their lives were no escape but an ever expanding commitment to the will of God. Those who want a quiet and undisturbed life are well advised to avoid taking prayer seriously, because to pray seriously is to deliver ourselves into the hands of God for him to do what he likes with us. All prayer is an echo of the prophet Isaiah:

'Here am I; send me.'

* * * * *

In saying that the test of the quality of our prayer is the quality of our living outside prayer, I do not mean that we should be constantly checking ourselves for virtue. There is another consideration at the heart of the gospel to be remembered here, and that is that as we come closer to God *it will appear to us* that we are further away! This paradox is to be found in all relationships of love, but especially in the love of God who is All Good and Pure. As we get closer in our hearts to him, the mediocrity of our own lives shows up more and more. We appear to ourselves to be sham and hollow, irretrievably mediocre. This is because the light of God is playing in our consciences and we become increasingly aware of how sinful and weak we are. The masks of our false selves are peeled away in the light of our meeting with God who is Truth. It is as if I were to bring the sleeve of my coat towards the window of the room and as I move into the light the dust and dandruff on the sleeve become more obvious. It is not that as I moved the coat got dirtier, but that the light got brighter. This experience is undergone by all who pray. They set out to serve God and paradoxically the sign that they are beginning to do this is that they realize how sinful they are, far from serving him properly. This can be discouraging until it is pointed out what is happening. We are now being identified with the true approach of the tax collector who could only beat his breast and ask for mercy, not with the false approach of the Pharisee who considered himself a worthy character. This experience is one reason why the Jesus Prayer is so helpful at this stage.

When I say that the test of prayer lies in our conduct, I do not mean that we ourselves should be the ones to judge it. This is best left to others, honest friends, wise guides, who are in a position to judge the generosity of our conduct and so to judge the generosity of our prayer. In doing so they will avoid the trap of judging by results, but look deeper for the quality of the effort put into our actions. In Christianity external success is a poor test of any action. The world's Redemption was effected by the colossal failure of Calvary, not the short-lived success of Palm Sunday. We who follow Christ need not look for that sense of well-being that comes from consciousness of a job well done. Comprehending and pleasing the infinite God in prayer is not within our powers. It is a task quite out of comparison with anything else we do. In it there will always be a sense of dissatisfaction, even guilt. This guilt is not the unhealthy or crippling kind which is based on unconscious fears. It is an entirely open and healthy guilt, which comes from consciously recognizing that we will never be able fully to please God or be perfect. There will always be a painful gap between our ideals and our achievements. It is a guilt which is accompanied by trust in a loving, understanding Father, a healing guilt which draws us closer to God's friendship. As we said before, Christianity is relational, not perfectionist. Christians can say with the poet, 'For us there is only the trying, the rest is not our business.' There is warmth and love in that truth, a warmth not to be found in the work ethic of much post-New Testament Christianity.

It can now be seen that the psychology of living the gospel is not an inner awareness of building up, but of demolition. The sign of progress in discipleship of Christ is a sharp feeling of being emptied out, not of being filled up. We are emptied out of that sense of having done well, that feeling of achievement which human beings like to possess in all they set their hands to. This is not to deny that often, under grace, we do achieve virtue and learn to pray well. The sense of failure comes from the fact that the standards given to us are now immeasurably high, and from the fact that we will never be a so good at imitating Christ and pleasing the Father as we should. The great saints were filled with this sense of failure, constantly presenting themselves as terrible sinners. This can be disconcerting to us who are not saints and we are tempted to disbelieve them, till we remember that they were close to God and so were seeing themselves under the divine light of truth. They were close to truth; it is we who are far from it. This sense of failure is, of course, given in prayer to make us depend on God more and realize the primary spiritual truth that we can do nothing of ourselves but all depends on him. Without that inner inadequacy we might become possessive about how we were doing and think we could manage without grace, on our own. It is, in fact, not so much a sense of failure but a sense of personal emptiness or non-possession. We may achieve something but we know it is because God is working through us, that we are simply vessels of God's grace, whose spiritual achievements are God's work, not ours.

How misplaced was the recent teaching of Catholic spirituality, with its emphasis on building up merit for oneself! It encouraged a spiritually possessive, mercantile mentality, alien from the gospel. It encouraged, by the offer of indulgences, a spirit of achievement, of reliance on merits, which kept people from understanding the gospel of poverty of spirit, and often kept them from trusting God. In our own day the true spirit of the gospel was shown by St Thérèse of Lisieux who, in a revolutionary way for her time, rejected the practice of spiritual merit hunting and frequently said that she wanted to appear at the end of her life 'empty-handed' before God. She was not interested in acquiring merit. She did not want to buy or negotiate her way into heaven. She wanted to throw herself upon the mercy of God and be saved by him. She is a great modern saint who called her age back to the gospel because she understood that in the Kingdom founded by Jesus Christ all is grace and gift, nothing is achievement. True Christian prayer is the royal, if painful, road to this truth.

9

Poverty Of Spirit

If, as we saw in the last chapter, a chief fruit of prayer is honesty about ourselves, the peeling away of that false sense of achievement to reveal our true self dependent on God, then an equally important fruit is growth in poverty of spirit. This too involves an unmasking, the unmasking this time of the hidden conditions, only partially known and acknowledged, in our surrender to God. Jesus warned his followers that not all those who said 'Lord, Lord' would enter the Kingdom of heaven. It is comparatively easy to profess our surrender to God with our lips. That is how we all begin – in prayer. If our prayer is serious, however, we will be led to see that the total surrender professed with our lips takes some time to permeate our whole lives. There is, when we first begin, a tendency to have reservations in this surrender, which are not fully conscious to ourselves. We are inclined to take away with one hand what we have first professed to give with the other. We will serve God, we say, as long as we have good health, or as long as we have people who understand us to work with, or as long as we are not asked to change the habits of a lifetime. These 'as long as' conditions are seldom explicit, usually just below the surface of our consciousness. But they are none the less real and operative in our lives. We are prepared to say no to God on these matters even before he should ask us to say yes and give up possession of them. What happens when we pray is that we are made blindingly and uncomfortably aware of this conditioned nature of our self-giving to God, our 'yes-but' attitude, and are faced with the need to eradicate it in order to be completely surrendered to God's will.

The challenge to surrender our conditions, reservations, towards God is the challenge of poverty of spirit – as long as we are making conditions in self-giving we are hoarding away riches in our life which are not given back to God. We are setting up supports in life, material or spiritual, on which to fall back if God's demands become too great. The invitation to poverty of spirit is the invitation to abandon all those attachments and be dependent on God's will alone. Poverty of spirit does not mean having no possessions, but having what we possess 'non-possessively,' entirely at God's behest, ready to give it up should it be taken. It is the invitation to possess things as *stewards*, not as absolute owners, the invitation to detachment. A good example from the Old Testament is Job, who was a rich man with all he wanted, property, a loving family, honour from his contemporaries, good health. When all those were taken from him, he accepted it, sitting among the ashes without property, family, honour or good health. 'The Lord gave and the Lord as taken away; blessed be the name of the Lord.' This reaction showed that even in the days of his prosperity Job was poor in spirit and possessed his goods as a steward of God, not as an absolute owner. Job was an all-weather friend of God, not merely a friend in times of prosperity. He was detached from all God had given him, not in the sense that he did not care about it, but in the sense that he was ready to have it taken from him without complaint.

Poverty of spirit can be seen as a condition of progress in prayer, something to be achieved in order that growth should come in prayer. It can also, however, be seen as a fruit of progress in prayer, something that happens to us as a sign that we have grown in contemplation. Put simply, what happens is that as, through prayer, God comes to be seen as the Absolute, the One Thing Necessary in our life, everything else comes to be seen as relative. The created world is recognized as good, created as it is by God, but it is viewed now in the light of God becoming absolute in our lives. It is seen as a beautiful and desirable, but relative and provisional. This does not take away from its importance, rather does it enhance it. But our relationship to these good things of creation undergoes a change. God has become more important to us, so they become less important or 'necessary' for us to be able to exist. If we were to lose them, like Job we could say: The Lord has given, the Lord takes away. This applies both to material things like food, drink, comfort, and to spiritual things like the support of friends or the devotional habits of our upbringing. In both cases progress in prayer has brought a certain detachment towards them in such a way that we can plot our growth in prayer through successive growth points in poverty of spirit. Each point of growth is a point where we have been challenged to let go our possessions happily, because in the light of God's love they are seen to be not needed and therefore dispensable. It is useful to enumerate these growth points, because by enumerating we can become aware of the challenge of contemplative prayer in a realistic way.

The area of the material good things of this world is an area for growth in the spiritual life. In this life we are surrounded by good things. They are not bad; they are gifts from God, created by him. So we must not be puritans, who forget the reality of Creation and Incarnation and condemn both the world and our humanity as bad. Spiritual growth does not come from condemning this world as bad but from seeing it as God-given, and therefore so precious that we must rigorously discipline ourselves to be non-possessive about it. This means letting go our desires to control, possess and use this world for ourselves – in other words, disciplining ourselves to be stewards of the good things of this life, administering them for God and our neighbour, not clinging to them in a proprietorial way. Here we have to be strict with ourselves if we want to grow spiritually. Here, as we grow in prayer and relate to God as our Absolute, we do find ourselves becoming less possessive and poorer in spirit.

Everyone will have his or her own list of good things over which to exercise special care to be non-possessive. All such lists will contain items like food, drink, material comfort, artificial heating in winter, cooling systems in summer. We must not cling to these; we must not turn them into necessities without which we cannot be ourselves. Consumer goods, too, should feature in the list: television, video machines, radios, cameras, tape recorders, books, cars, clothes, the furnishings of our homes. The commercial society in which most of us live has a vested interest in making our lives revolve round these goods in order to make us spending much money on them. Our society would like us to find our identity in our possessions, would like to define us by our 'having' not our 'being.' When God becomes absolute in our lives, consumer goods become relative. We find we can do without them to a degree which we had not previously guessed and which spells bad news for the world of commerce. All who dedicate themselves to God in prayer find that they become independent of consumer goods. Whether they have them or not, they are free from the need to possess them; they can travel light through life in the midst of the glittering plenty of the industrialized world. We need look no further than Jesus Christ for an example of this material independence. He enjoyed the things of this world but manifestly did not depend on them – he was a man you could not define in terms of having, only in terms of being.

A second area of liberation from dependence is the less tangible area of spiritual possessions. We all 'possess' certain immaterial things which give us joy and satisfaction. Our job, the office we hold, our status and good image in the eyes of others, our reputation, power – these are some of the intangible goods which we are given in life. They are intangible, not material like food or houses, but we cling to them with greater tenacity than we do material things, for after all they are more desirable and valuable to us. Who, for instance, will not cling to his or her reputation immeasurably more closely than to money or comfort? Once again, however, our progress in prayer can be gauged by the

generosity with which we let go in these areas. 'The
Lord gives; the Lord takes away.' As the Lord becomes more
absolute to us, so our hold over these things lessens till we
reach the stage of not caring about them, or rather, caring
about them under the will and good pleasure of God. They
are seen to be relative in our life. We act as stewards of these
gifts from God, not as absolute owners. It is important,
especially, to be a steward and not an absolute owner of
power.

In the area of spirituality, in particular, we have to learn to
let go if we are to grow. Our spiritual life is replete with
devotional props: places, persons, images, devotions, cus-
toms, practices, which help us maintain contact with God.
We need these aids. Few, if any, can have a relationship with
the invisible God without them. Nevertheless, as we saw in
earlier chapters, there comes a time for all of us when we are
invited to throw away these aids, like a cured patient
throwing away his crutches. This moment is the moment
when to cling to them would be to refuse a direct, simple
contact with God in favour of the more familiar, apparently
safer, attachment to our devotions. This is, in George
Herbert's comparison, to continue to look lovingly at the
window instead of looking lovingly at the view through the
window. Even the most inspiring devotions can obscure our
view of God, if we stay with them too long. As Abbot
Blosius said, 'Not only bad things, but even those that are
good, may become hindrances if they are loved and sought
inordinately, just as plates of gold held before the eyes
prevent sight as effectively as plates of iron.' As always,
resurrection in spiritual things only comes about after

death. The immature, often easy, devotional approach of beginners must die before a more mature, simple approach is born. We act as stewards of the gifts of God, not possessors, so must be ready to surrender them when God desires. This applies, even, to spiritual gifts which we thought were our treasures for life, like a favourite devotion or a hallowed liturgical practice. Here, too, God may call us to be dispossessed in the interests of our love for him.

The third area where God the Dispossessor may be at work is the area of human support. One of the fundamental needs of human beings, if they are to be psychologically healthy, is for affirmation and acceptance by the community they live in. It is as necessary for them as food for the body. In fact it *is* food: psychological nourishment which enables them to be healthy as persons, capable of real relationships with others, not stunted in their personhood. To be accepted and supported is the desired aim of community living, bringing social and personal fulfillment. Once again, this is why we must not cling possessively to it. It may become a plate of gold held before our eyes. Maturity, then, means that we will be asked to do without this human support at the time when to cling to it would prevent our growth and obscure our route to God. There is always the danger that we will make being accepted warmly by others the absolute aim of our life; whereas it must remain a relative aim, something which may be given to us by God at one time and be taken away at another. In practice this means that we must not cling possessively to the following good things, but must remain grateful, contented but unattached: other people's esteem, their notice, their thanks, their understanding, their support, their encouragement, their respect – in a word, community affirmation. All these form the staple diet of any community, but staple diet which God will not allow us to turn into an idol, and so may starve us of it for our own good, in the interests of spiritual growth. This starvation is in order to help us purify our motives. We must train ourselves to be detached from the human supports in order to centre our lives on God. The test is whether we can work hard the Christian cause without looking for thanks, or recognition, or even success. If we can, it means we are working for the pure motive of God's glory, unmixed with lesser self-centred motives. This process of purification is a necessary stage in the journey towards true poverty of spirit. People who live in community should remember this truth. Today there is a real desire for authentic community both among the traditional religious orders and in the new lay communes which have become widespread. My impression is that in communities today the need for social affirmation is sometimes placed above the duty to serve God, with the result that spiritual growth stops, to be replaced by a psychological softness which elevates needs beyond duties. When that happens a community becomes sadly inward-looking, existing primarily for itself, and paradoxically becoming less happy. In God's will only is our peace to be found, not in the search for love and affirmation.

In Christianity the good is enemy of the best. Good food, human comfort, physical health are good things which may have to be forgone at times of spiritual challenge. It is the same with this very helpful psychological gift of social affirmation. That, too, may have to be done without so that we may grow towards God and be independent of community groups. All leaders have to learn to act without support and not be dependent on it. You cannot be a pioneer in any field unless you have learned to be faced with lack of understanding, even hostility, and live through the experience creatively and without bitterness. The maturity required is that of being ready and able to give up these good things in favour of acquiring the best, which is union with God. In biblical terms, the journey to the fulfillment of the Promised Land lies through the desert. Exodus has to be undergone, perhaps for many years in the desert, before we are sufficiently purified to meet God in the Promised Land.

Jesus said, 'Seek first the Kingdom, and all else will be given unto you.' He does not ask us to cultivate an impassive indifference in life. He knows we are human beings as he was, and therefore needing to be passionately concerned and anxious about things. To be concerned, anxious and passionate is to be human. It is not something to be ashamed of, but something to rejoice in. To be without desires, a passionless pudding, is inhuman. Jesus was human, so he does not ask his followers to deny their desires. What he does is to redirect those desires. Jesus directs our anxieties towards the true object of human aspirations, the only one which will fulfill them. This he called the Father's Will, or the Kingdom of God. Jesus' gospel says: Strive fully after that; be thoroughly anxious about that; exercise all your human endeavour towards that. When you do so, you will find that you have little anxiety left for the things most people are anxious about in our consumer-oriented world. You will become less bothered about material comfort, spiritual gifts, social acceptance. Your strivings in that direction will diminish and fade. You will discover a pure beauty in Christ's Kingdom which at first was not visible to you. Then you will discover that same beauty in the world, a beauty which you can fully enjoy because you are not now striving anxiously to possess it. It is there simply to enjoy for its own sake, and to give glory to God. No wonder Jesus called his message Good News. It is good news to be told how to live in this beautiful world and love it properly.

10

Liberation

Liberation is a word much used in Christian circles today. This is hardly surprising, since liberation or redemption is that central message of the New Testament. Jesus Christ is Saviour, Redeemer or Liberator, depending on one's vocabulary. Liberation can have two separate meanings: freedom from external restraint and freedom from internal compulsions. The two are closely connected, but do not necessarily go together. When speakers talk about the need to liberate the oppressed peoples of the world, those with no political freedom, those imprisoned and tortured for their beliefs, the enormous number of our fellow human beings suffering from economic exploitation, living in the slavery of poverty and squalor, they are talking about external freedom. Liberation theology is largely concerned with that freedom, which is the birthright of all human beings, but which, devastatingly, is denied to the majority of them.

Internal freedom is a separate matter. This is also the birthright of all men and women, and it too is not won without a struggle. Internal freedom is freedom not from a tyranny imposed on us by others but from the tyranny of ourselves, our uncurbed passions and desires which enslave us no less really than the secret police of an oppressive regime. An example of a liberated person in the internal sense is a reformed alcoholic. He or she has won a liberation after, perhaps, years of humiliating slavery, a liberation which has taken place deep down inside and which is very real.

I think the best way to describe the connection between the two kinds of liberation is to see them as both part of the Christian gospel, both goals to be sought by Christians, and to see them as parallel aims. One goal of the follower of Christ is freedom for all from external tyrannies. The other goal is the internal freedom which for the Christian only comes from communion with Christ. In terms of priority, this second goal is more important, according to the gospel, even though in terms of time external liberation comes first. You do not speak to a prisoner about internal peace. You free him. The urgency of the New Testament writers is for the second, deeper, freedom. There is little urgency for the first freedom. Slaves, for instance, are told to obey their masters, good or bad, thereby imitating Jesus in his passion (1 Peter 2:18–25). The early Church left the struggle against slavery to a later date. It concentrated its urgency on the immediate struggle in the heart of every person against sin. St Paul gives a classic description of the inner slavery of the second kind, the slavery we all undergo when our wayward desires are not yet brought under the control of grace. Most readers will be able to identify with this passage: 'I do not understand my own actions. For I do not do what I want, but I do the very thing I hate ... For I know that nothing good dwells within me, that is, in my flesh. I can will what is right, but I cannot do it. For I do not do the

good I want, but the evil I do not want is what I do'
(Romans 7:15–19). We do not have to be alcoholics or drug
addicts but simply average sinful Christians to recognize
that as an accurate description of our internal struggles to
keep our resolutions and remain faithful to grace. The gift
which God will give us, as he gave St Paul, is the gift of
grace, which brings with it a liberation from this tyranny of
the 'flesh,' our unredeemed human nature. This liberation
is one of the fruits of prayer, which comes with poverty of
spirit.

In the last chapter we described poverty of spirit as what
happens when, through prayer, we realize God to be the
Absolute in our lives, with the result that all else becomes
obviously relative. This is a liberation: a liberation from the
natural acquisitiveness in us all, which makes us work so
hard to gain possessions. When we have no divine Absolute
in our lives, all manner of created things become absolute
by turns to us. A new car, a new kitchen, new clothes, new
equipment for entertainment – these increasingly fill our
hearts until we become victims to the 'I want, I have'
mentality, which is the salesman's dream and which, if
uncontrolled, will lead us into a crazy chase which never
brings satisfaction. It is indeed a liberation to be freed from
this chase by the life of prayer.

Another way of describing this liberation by poverty of
spirit is to say that we gradually become more inner-
directed. The values we live by, and which are important to
us, become internalized. At first, the values most people live
by are external to themselves. They achieve a feeling of
well-being through their work and their possessions. What

makes them 'feel OK,' free from insecurity, is the work they do, with all the labour and sweat that goes into it, and the acquired possessions with which they surround themselves. These two factors help them to take their place in society and face their fellow human beings with confidence. They are socially dependent on them; to be unemployed and poor would be crippling and would give them no identity in society; their confidence would drain away. For the Christian this should not be so. The journey to maturity for the Christian is precisely the journey from externalized values (doing, having) to the state where the values that matter are wholly internal (being). The Christian is invited to find his or her identity ('to feel OK') simply from being an adopted child of God, simply from being loved by the Father, whatever the external circumstances of life, employed or unemployed, poor or rich. It is easy to put this on paper. It is not so easy to achieve. Like most gifts of God this liberation is at first sight a frightening one.

When I was in the course of writing this book I suffered two heart attacks which landed me in the hospital followed by a length convalescence. Thus I passed abruptly from the busy life of a pastor in a city parish, each day filled from morning to evening with activities among diverse people and innumerable tasks to be done, to the life of an idle convalescent by the fireside. Every day now stretched out before me with no task to perform and I was often puzzled how to fill it. I would take an hour to read the daily newspaper which before I had hurriedly skipped through between pastoral tasks. This abrupt change from doing to simply being helped me to see that in God's eyes what matters is who we, his children, are and not what we do, still less how much we possess. By surrendering myself to God's adorable will I was able to find my true identity, and not worry about whether I was inactive or active, busy or idle. My true self below the surface level of activities was united with God deep down within me. I was liberated from the need to be busy and simply found myself in God. 'In his will is our peace.'

* * * * *

Another aspect of the inner liberation which surrender to God brings can best be expressed in the word availability. Being available to people is an important side to loving them. It underlines that element of receptivity in love of which we spoke in an earlier chapter. Too often we think that to show love for our neighbour means to be busy, almost interfering, in their lives. That is indeed a significant part of love, but the other aspect of being available to our neighbour, allowing him and her to interfere in our lives, is equally important. The better test of love is not whether we have been active in our neighbours' lives but whether we have been receptive, been good listeners at inconvenient moments, allowed them to give us unwanted advice, given them *time*. All this means self-discipline, the self-discipline of surrendering the desire to be in charge of events, so as to allow others to give one orders, upset one's life, threaten one's privacy. Once again it is a question of inner liberation, the achievement of freedom from the need always to be in command of situations. I am only completely free when I am ready for others to enter into my life at a time of their choosing, not mine, and can do this without internal insecurity, being perfectly ready for whoever or whatever the Lord may send. It goes without saying that this freedom is an essential ingredient of the pastoral life in the parish. The good pastor, or shepherd, is not he who can only be approached at stated times, but he who is willing to be interrupted at all times by his flock and loves them for it.

It is not only people to whom we must be hospitable. It is also ideas. Most of us feel more threatened by new, revolutionary ideas which call in question our way of life than by people who importune us. We can usually summon the strength to be hospitable to people without too much fear. It is not easy to welcome new, challenging ideas about our faith without giving in to fear. Yet hospitality to new ideas is also part of the freedom which prayer brings. When I say hospitality I do not mean that we must necessarily agree with every new idea that is floated. Whether we agree or not is a question of rational argument and decision. By hospitality I mean the willingness to listen to new ideas objectively without fear. Without that initial willingness to listen there can be no advance as far as rational argument and rational acceptance or rejection. In the generation we live in in the Church we have had plenty of opportunity to be tested in this matter. We have had a succession of new ideas and movements in the Church since Vatican II. Some have been accepted by the official Church (like vernacular liturgy), others are still under discussion (like women priests). Not all of us have come out well from the challenge. Many, even those in positions of authority in the Church, have not been able to overcome their fears and have run away from a cool assessment of the new ideas into something akin to panic. The inner freedom from fear of new things has been lacking. To put it more positively, the inner trust in God, who guides his Church and protects it from error, has been lacking. Surrender to God in prayer and poverty of spirit could help us face all new things in the Church, if we have the courage to follow that course.

* * * * *

The final point in our lives of surrender to God in prayer is that serene condition of mind and heart which the philosophers of old aimed to achieve in one way or another, but which inevitably for them became the pursuit of the leisured, aristocratic classes, by no means the expected goal of ordinary people. In Christianity it is not an achievement, but a gift – the gift of intimacy with God which through prayer brings serenity and contentment. It is therefore a gift for all, not just for a chosen few. There is, in fact, a wide gap between the goal of detached serenity of the ancient philosophers, which was essentially impersonal and self-centred, and the joy of the Christian saints who found contentment not by cultivating it as a direct aim, but by devoting their lives to Jesus Christ and seeking first his Kingdom. For Christians joy and peace come as 'spin-offs' from their main goal (the Kingdom of God) not as their direct aim. Writing to the Philippians St Paul recognizes that his contentment and joy came from Christ:

> 'I have learnt in whatever state I am, to be content. I
> know how to be abased, and I know how to abound;
> in any and all circumstances I have learnt the secret

of facing plenty and hunger, abundance and want. I can do all things in him who strengthens me.' (Phil 4:11–13)

The particular strength that Christ brings us is the strength enshrined in his saying: 'Where your treasure is, there your heart will be.' The fact that our treasure is to be found secure in God himself and not insecurely in the passing events of this life means that, as long as we keep our hearts fixed on that treasure, we will not be anxious. Depending on where their treasures are, men and women are anxious or peaceful. The miser's treasure is money, a notoriously shifting commodity; so he can never be peaceful, must always be anxious. Those who set their hearts on being popular with their fellow human beings are even less peaceful than the miser, because social popularity is even more shifting and like quick-silver. Consequently lives devoted to achieving it are frantic and desperate in the pursuit, and so easily become dependent on falsehood and subterfuge, as we know from the public relations industry employed by politicians and industrialists. Politicians are among the least serene and contented of human beings. Their treasures are inevitably placed in extremely vulnerable receptacles like public opinion or market forces.

I do not want to be too glib in talking about the serenity and joy which comes from placing all our trust in God. It is never easy to be at peace deep down when the surface of our lives is in turmoil. The lives of the saints, however, show us that with help from God it can be done. On the surface most of their lives were afflicted with trouble. For instance, St Francis of Assisi was deprived of the leadership of the Friars Minor, his own creation. St Thomas More was removed from the Lord Chancellorship of England and imprisoned in the Tower of London. At one level these extremely human men must have been in agony and turmoil; but at the deeper level they maintained an utter serenity and peace, and were able to be joyful and even to make jokes as they went to their death. Let the last word of this chapter belong to the puritan John Milton, afflicted with blindness towards the end of his life. He, too, exhibited the joyful serenity of a man given completely to God, a man whose perspective was right because his treasure was beyond the ambitions of this world.

> 'To be blind is not misery; it is misery not to be able to endure blindness ... Through this infirmity I can be completed, perfected; in this darkness I can be filled with light. For in truth we blind men are not God's last and slightest care; in proportion as we cannot behold anything except himself, he is disposed to look upon us with the more mercy and kindness.'

Towards Union

11

Dark Night

A book on prayer would not be complete without at least a short chapter on the phenomenon writers call the Dark Night. This phrase, coined by St John of the Cross, should not be regarded too anxiously, in spite of its flavour of drama, because in reality it describes a very humdrum and ordinary series of events which is met by the everyday virtue of perseverance and does not call for unusually dramatic measures. An explanation will make that clear.

Dark Night describes twin happenings in the Christian life of prayer as we develop and mature. The first happening is that the effective initiative in our spiritual lives passes from our hands over to God. The second is that God when he takes this initiative allows us to suffer, especially in prayer. Although it is clearly foolish to pretend to know God's mind so well that one can explain why he does things to everyone's satisfaction, nevertheless it is possible to study the good effects the Dark Night has in our souls, and so analyse how God allows these things to happen for our own ultimate good. This chapter attempts to do that and no more.

The path to spiritual maturity was traced by Jesus in his words to Peter after the Resurrection:

'Truly, truly, I say to you, when you were young, you girded yourself and walked where you would; but when you are old you will stretch out your hands, and another will gird you and carry you where you do not wish to go.' (Jn 21:18)

Spiritual growth, then, is not as we might expect, a journey towards gaining complete control of one's life, but on the contrary, a journey towards being less in control of one's destiny, more at the mercy of others, because deep down surrendered to God. The condition of being in control of one's destiny is the condition of the young apostle, who girds himself and goes where he wants to. The mature apostle must expect others to gird him and take him where he does not want to go. But it will not be a hijacking; Peter will allow it to happen; he will 'stretch out his hand' and be surrendered to God's will in the matter. In other words, spiritual maturity will be a growth in that willed receptivity to God's actions which we have already seen is at the heart of true prayer.

This loss of initiative in one's Christian life and corresponding growth in receptivity is what St John of the Cross meant by the Passive Dark Night. He argued that as long as a person was 'in charge' of his or her spiritual life, was at the helm, making the plans and giving the orders, there was a danger of swelling pride and vanity. Someone taking to religion in all zeal, becoming caught up in a campaign of prayer, fasting, spiritual reading, liturgical practice, retreat weekends, might be indulging unawares in one big ego-trip. The truly genuine religious zeal might be having a long-term adverse effect by swelling the vanity and self-centredness of the Christian insidiously in the name of religion. The zeal of the convert, not yet tried by adversity, could well lead away from God instead of close to him. As St John put it, the conversion of the soul from a worldly life to a spiritual life is at first superficial only. The convert has been given new, spiritual goals; but the conversion is only external; in itself the soul is as full as it ever was of unregenerate tendencies to vanity, arrogance, acquisitiveness, the only difference being that after conversion these tendencies are now attached to spiritual instead of worldly objects. The new convert is as acquisitive as he always was, but he is acquisitive for spiritual goods like grace and merit; he is as arrogant as ever, but his arrogance is now 'for God,' not 'for self.' This is shrewd observation. We have all met the religious enthusiast for prayer, or liturgy, or some movement in the Church. The zeal is infectious, but it is, as yet, chiefly the expression of the person's vanity or self-centredness, dressed up in Christian clothes. We know that that person will have to undergo a few knocks, experience a few failures, before he or she is converted in the heart to God. Those knocks and failures, the guiding by another and being taken where one does not want to go, are what St John called the Dark Night.

The growth process does not happen automatically. It is possible that the knocks and failures may turn the enthusiast off religion, in which case there is an end to all progress. It depends on the response to the hardships and failures. If the response is generous, the failures are taken as part of God's plan. Then the maturing process will be under way.

In other words, the therapy of the Dark Night is not so much the suffering sent by God as the reaction we make to it (with God's grace). We have to 'stretch out our hands' and be cooperative, otherwise there is no freedom and so no growth. In a nutshell, if we persevere through the sufferings, we will grow towards God. If we do not, we fall backwards. That wise counsellor the Curé d'Ars said, 'One hour of patience is worth several days of fasting.' Fasting is hard, but it is my initative and choice and so, paradoxically, may effect a growth in my native self-will. I may become pleased with my achievement. Patience is much harder; I am not in charge; self-will is being punctured; all I have to do is persevere, which is not a very glamorous activity; there is little danger of pride; probably I will be humiliated as I discover how impatient I am; through the humiliation of not being in charge of what happens and the discovery of my impatience I will unspectacularly grow in God's grace.

A good instance of this pattern of growth is in the realm of prayer. At first for most of us prayer goes well. Many readers will have experienced the growing intimacy and ease of communication with God which I outlined in the first three chapters of this book. Such simplicity in prayer is experienced as a grace from God, completely undeserved but wonderful. Then comes the testing period. Prayer stops being easy and perceptibly intimate. It becomes difficult to persevere; God seems far away, not near; God even seems absent, and prayer a mockery. Prayer becomes a hard grind, not an easy ride. Perhaps the predominant experience at this time is that of discovering prayer to be boring. This is a humiliating discovery and one that, in view of earlier protestations of joy and wonder in prayer, people often want to keep quiet about because they are ashamed. The best thing to do at this point is to consult a neutral observer with knowledge of the ways of prayer. He or she will first ascertain if this stoppage in prayer is caused by any fault in the person praying, e.g. a double life of unrepented sin and prayer, or lack of effort. Should this be so, the remedy is clear. Once taken, the path of prayer is open again.

Far more often, however, blockage in prayer is not because of any fault of one's own. It is simply because of the Dark Night. God wants us to grow deeper and more persevering; so he sends us this surface dryness in prayer. The remedy is to persevere; in the act of continuing to pray, even when on the surface it is arid and God seems to be absent, lies the solution. We are forced to touch God less in our emotions, more in faith. We dip below the surface of gratification of the emotion, and discover God in the convictions of faith, hope and love. God *seems* to our surface self to be absent, but in faith we believe him to be present. In the persevering prayer of faith, often utterly unrewarding on the surface, we contact him. After some months of this persevering (not with gritted teeth but trustingly), we find that we have been given a great grace by God. We can contact him in prayer by faith, whether we 'feel' him to be present or not. We are no longer dependent on emotional returns in our prayer life. Like Job we can say about feelings in prayer, 'The Lord gave, the Lord has taken away; blessed be the name of the Lord.' Having learnt this lesson, it is then an added joy when emotional sweetness comes back in prayer, since dryness does not last for ever.

The point of the Dark Night is not that we should value dryness as in itself a good thing, which it is not. The point is that we should value the lesson it teaches us.

St John of the Cross discerns two levels in the human person where this therapeutic blockage is at work. The first level is that of the emotions and visible results, the level we have been examining in the matter of prayer. To this level belongs everything that can be classified as 'religion', that is, the human response, both personal and ecclesiastical, to God's approach to us. Over the years Christian tradition has constructed a huge edifice of religion, an impressive corpus of religious response to God. It ranges from public liturgical practices and sacramental symbols to all the private devotions and aids to prayer which we savour personally and find so helpful. To these I would also add all that is found in those thriving sections of all bookstores today: the 'how to' books on personal fulfillment. These books, which have such an appeal to modern western men and women, belong to the category of religion, the man-made response to God and life. When followed they evoke a busy religious activity, and many Christians read them. In this sphere the Dark Night operates as a blockage, taking the form of distaste for all these activities of religion. But the blockage is therapeutic, leading the devotees of religious practices to see below the surface delights in order to contact God directly in faith. For instance, the liturgical enthusiast is taught, through the fairly shattering experience of sudden distaste for all liturgy, to handle liturgical worship properly, and be fascinated no longer by the transient forms but by God himself. This temporary 'death of liturgy' in the soul of its devotee is often the birth of true worship in that soul. Looking through the glass of the window he is confronted with God in a direct manner, perhaps for the first time, and so no longer lingers on the shape and beauty of the window. He has learnt to put liturgy and religion in their true perspective of faith. We gather in church to worship God, not to experience liturgy.

The second level in the human person at which the Dark Night operates is that deeper level of purpose and direction in life. It is the level in us at which we are most ourselves, precisely the level which is strengthened in faith when the surface, religious level is blocked. If the former level can be characterized as the area of religion, then this level belongs to faith. Here too God is therapeutically at work and allows a 'death'. We find that the movements of the spirit which relate us directly to God, those of faith, trust, love, become themselves subject to doubt. We start to wonder if we really believe in God, after all. This effectively knocks away the foundation of our life up to now. If we do not believe in God it makes no sense to trust him or to love him. There seems to be nothing left to us which can be called Christian or spiritual. Is there any point in going on? This second Dark Night is considerably more disturbing and painful than the earlier surface one, since it threatens us at the root of all we believe in and stand for. There is not much that can be said about it, since words are not much use here. A detached observer can explain that this experience is God's way of strengthening our faith, by the paradoxical way of threatening to destroy it, so that we have to exercise it more than ever before. Our reaction to the night and the darkness in the depth of our being is to make renewed, 'blind,' acts of faith and trust in God. A book like this can comment clinically on God's design, but the experience itself is far from detached. You cannot say to yourself: this is God's design, all is well, because you are in the process of doubting whether God exists and whether there is such a design. Christianity appears to be a fairy tale, with any number of psychological explanations. You feel you have deceived yourself about God and about prayer, that any experiences you may have had in the past were self-induced, perhaps escape mechanisms to justify not getting involved in the world of action. The whole 'God business' appears a hollow sham. Yet you plod on in bewilderment, believing against belief, and hoping against hope. The reward, when it is all over, is strengthened faith and hope, strengthened Christian purpose.

These two night experiences in the soul are usually described in a chronological sequence: first, the testing of religion and all the 'how to' problems of spirituality; next, the testing of faith and the 'whether' questions concerning God, Christ and the Church. While there is truth in this sequence, it is perhaps preferable to talk of a spiral progress. We go in and out of these experiences, and often after many years find ourselves back to the problems we first started with, with the feeling that we have made no progress. In one sense we have indeed come back to the beginning, but it can be observed that we are now beginning again at a deeper level. Our progress has been spiral, going over the same ground monotonously and apparently learning nothing, but each time somehow going deeper, spiralling down in our journey to the depths.

The biblical metaphor which is used to describe the spiritual experiences which I have delineated in this chapter is Desert. It takes its origin from the archetypal liberation experience of the Israelites, the Exodus from Egypt. You can observe the spiritual experiences of growth at work in the People of God during the Exodus. They were liberated from slavery to the fleshpots of Egypt into the Desert, but once they were there, they hated it. Freedom in the Desert was not as appealing to them as slavery in Egypt. 'O that we had meat to eat! We remember the fish we ate in Egypt for nothing, the cucumbers, the melons, the leeks, the onions, and the garlic; but now our strength is dried up, and there is nothing at all but this manna to look at' (Numbers 11: 4–6). The greatness of Moses was that he resisted these popular demands and kept the Israelites in the Desert, until out of that experience all their strengths were born. They met God at Sinai and were forged into his People, with the Law and the Covenant, to give them thereafter their unbreakable conviction that they had a destiny, which was God-given. After the Exodus they were God's Chosen People. In spite of falterings they never looked back. It took a lifetime in the Desert, however, to fashion them into thinking that way.

God tests us as he tested his People in the Desert. He asks us to grow beyond the appeals to instant gratification (cucumbers, melons, leeks, onions and garlic) which assail us from all sides in our society. He asks us to pray at a deeper level than the expectation of instant results, to follow Christ without social support or 'stroking' from anyone, in fact to take up the cross in our discipleship. He asks us to face the experience of Desert, because he knows that it is in the Desert that we become his spouses, not among the Egyptian fleshpots. That was how Jeremiah saw the Exodus: as God leading his bride into the Desert in order to marry her there (Jeremiah 2:2). God wants us to be as firm and faithful to him as he is to us. The Desert is the place where we learn that lesson. An Arab saying is apt: 'The Desert is no place for a man who is afraid to meet his God. The Desert is the Garden of Allah.' You have, however, to go there to discover that.

12

Cloud Of Unknowing

Anyone who reflects about God and how he has revealed himself to us in the Old and New Testaments soon realizes that we can only know God *through human terms*. There is no special language, special unique words, which are reserved only for talking about God and which we do not use for the rest of human life. On the contrary all the words we use about God come from our human experience. Especially, the words of the revealed Bible are entirely culled from life in this world. God reveals himself as *compassionate*, or *loving*, or *powerful*. Jesus revealed him as *Our Father*. There is nothing said about God in Old or New Testament which is not couched in thoroughly human language. It has long been the realization, therefore, that when we talk about God in this everyday human language, we have to remember to make a mental correction. Thus, we say that God is compassionate, but we must immediately remember that God's compassion is infinitely greater, is qualitatively quite other, than any example of human compassion from which we derive our understanding of the term. If we do not make this mental correction we fall into the trap of anthropomorphism, of making God in a human image. To put it in another way, we have no special language in which to talk about God, therefore we have to use ordinary, human language in a *special way*. God is just, but in a special divine way far beyond human justice, which we can never hope to comprehend completely. God is our Father, but in a way which completely transcends any human father's way of being father. All these human words used about God are only approximations, not untrue, but certainly not containing the whole truth about the Divine Nature, which in this life we will never know.

The above paragraph can be understood by any Christian who pauses for a moment to reflect on the matter. He or she does not have to engage in prayer to see this truth about 'God-talk.' What happens when we pray is that we not only see it as a detached truth, but we feel it as a personal sorrow. In prayer we reach out to God, longing to grasp him in knowledge and love, but we come up against this infinite gap, which we cannot cross. We feel baffled. We feel frustrated. We feel sore. The Being to whom we have dedicated ourselves in prayer, whom we want to know above all others, remains hidden from us. Furthermore we know that he will go on being hidden; we will never know God in this life, however many hours we devote to prayer or reading. In this life we will never see him face to face; it will always be a meeting 'in glass, darkly.' The hiddenness of God will be an ever-present element in our prayer. A lifetime of prayer which does not attain its Object stretches out before us. It is tempting to abandon prayer at this point on the grounds that we have been fooled: the more we pray, the more we are baffled by 'unknowing' God. It is the opposite of what we could have expected.

There are many descriptions of this state of contemplative bafflement in spiritual literature. The one which helps me most is the simple medieval English one of 'cloud of unknowing.' According to the anonymous author of this 14th century book, when one prays one is drawn into a cloud, in which all one's previous clear concepts about God break down, and one is left only with *unknowing*. One does not, never will, know God, because all those human terms referred to him are inadequate. One is invited to stay in this cloud, as it were, beating against the barrier which blocks one from God, knowing it will never be crossed. Moreover the poverty-stricken state of the contemplative in the cloud of unknowing is further compounded by the fact that he has deliberately, during prayer, excluded the created world from his thoughts so as to concentrate upon God. In the words of the author, he has put the created world behind him in a 'cloud of forgetting,' while in front of him, between himself and God is a cloud of unknowing. He is caught between the two 'clouds,' one of his own deliberate making in order to reach God better, the other apparently of God's making to prevent him coming too close! He finds himself, during prayer, in a barren no-man's-land, with no crumbs of comfort for his questing mind or imagination. It is the country of faith, St Paul's dark glass, not the country of vision, the sight of God's glory.

At this stage the important thing is to rejoice, not to give way to sadness or sulks. We must rejoice because we are advancing in Truth. Although it is painful, the bafflement we experience is a dose of truth for our minds. We are discovering that no human being can know God. We can know that he exists, but not what he is like. If we are honest we have to confess that up to this point, we did think we knew what God was like. All those descriptions in the Bible, especially the psalms, convinced us that we could build up a picture of what God was like. Now we realize that, in doing that, we were falling into the trap of anthropomorphism – in fact, of idolatry: of fashioning God according to a human image: a great Big Daddy for our needs. The advance we have been allowed to make in prayer has taken the form of a smashing of some of those personal idols.

The constant danger of idolatry vis à vis God that human beings risk is neatly pin-pointed in an early poem of W.B. Yeats:

> 'I passed along the water's edge below the
> humid trees,
> My spirit rocked in evening light, the rushes
> round my knees,
> My spirit rocked in sleep and sighs; and saw
> the moor-fowl pace
> All dripping on a grassy slope, and saw them
> cease to chase
> Each other round in circles, and heard the
> eldest speak:
> *Who holds the world between His bill and made*
> *us strong or weak*
> *Is an undying moorfowl, and He lives beyond*
> *the sky.*
> *The rains are from His dripping wing, the*
> *moonbeams from His eye.*

I passed a little further on and heard a lotus
talk;
Who made the world and ruleth it, He hangeth
on a stalk,
For I am in His image made, and all this
tinkling tide
Is but a sliding drop of rain between His petals
wide.
A little way within the gloom a roebuck raised
his eyes
Brimful of starlight, and he said: *The Stamper*
of the Skies,
He is a gentle roebuck; for how else, I pray, could
he
Conceive a thing so sad and soft, a gentle thing
like me?
I passed a little further on and heard a
peacock say:
Who made the grass and made the worms and
made my feathers gay,
He is a monstrous peacock, and He waveth all
the night
His languid tail above us, lit with myriad spots
of light.'

In other words, just as for a vegetable God could be por-
trayed as an unimaginably marvellous Vegetable, for birds
an unimaginably marvellous Bird and for animals an unimaginably marvellous Animal, so untrained human beings
will tend to think of God as a marvellous, supernatural

Person, ruling over them from heaven. The experience of the cloud of unknowing cures us of that. It is cause for rejoicing that we have been delivered from the danger of idolatry in prayer, and that in our lives the truth is beginning to emerge, however dry and painful the experience may be.

One of the lessons which our sojourn in the cloud of unknowing teaches us is the lesson which has already been dwelt upon in this book, that we cannot hope to master God. He masters us. As we have already noticed, people setting out upon the venture of prayer often have an unconscious assumption that they are about to master the subject, learn the rules, become competent in prayer. It comes as a shock to them when the opposite happens: they do not master God; they cannot even know him; they do not feel satisfied, but contrariwise naggingly dissatisfied; they find themselves painfully incompetent. This is the lesson of the cloud of unknowing. It is bound up with many of our assumptions about God, that he is kind, compassionate, will always 'stroke' us. But God does not necessarily fall in with our assumptions about him. He can be quite tough with those who love him. He can, at times, offer no consolations or rewards. As Archbishop Bloom expresses it, 'God is not a pussy cat.' He is not cosy. One of the ways, for instance, in which we learn that is in our understanding of God's justice. Many people approach God with pre-arranged notions about his justice. It is often a sharp shock to them to discover that God is sometimes not in the least just by human standards! He does not reward his servants with good things; he allows mothers with young children to die of cancer; he allows the wicked to prosper; he does not always crown virtue with reward; he is far beyond our comprehension. This lesson is again part of the experience of the cloud of unknowing. We thought we knew God, but now find that he is far more of a mystery than we imagined. His thoughts and ways are not the same as mankind's thoughts and ways. He is beyond our comprehension. He is a mystery. When we grasp that, we often find we can return to the gospel and understand it better than before. The mysteries in the pages of the New Testament fall into place better, once we have prayed our way into the cloud of unknowing.

Stranded in the cloud of unknowing, we continue to pray. The experience has, of course, a marked effect on how we pray. We become chary of placing too much dependence on words, knowing, as we do, that words are only finite expressions of infinite truths. The beautiful words of the psalms, for instance, continue to be most expressive of our attitudes to God, but as descriptions of God and his attitude to us we regard them with a new caution; they are true, but not the whole truth. So we turn to silence. Silence becomes the richest and best way of praying in the cloud of unknowing. It is our almost automatic reaction to the discovery that God is Mystery. We become speechless before the mystery of God and of Jesus Christ.

For human beings to become speechless is seldom evidence that we are empty; nearly always it is evidence that we are 'too full.' If I become speechless with anger over something it is not because I have nothing to say, but because I have too much to say and no word in my vocabulary is adequate to express my rage. So I stand speechless, too full of anger to be able to express it. I am struck dumb. We can find ourselves at a loss for words in the throes of many different emotions. We can be struck dumb before a feast laid out on a table, not knowing where to begin. We can be speechless with wonder before a work of art or a view. Above all we can be reduced to silence in love. In chapter two I described how the progress of two people from the state of being strangers to each other to that of being friends was also a progress towards being able to be silent and relaxed in each other's company. The third stage, which I am now describing, is when two people are so much in love with each other that they do not want to talk; words would get in the way; silence is the only way they can express their love for each other. They adore each other in mutual wordlessness.

That is how the relationship between the soul and God in the cloud of unknowing develops. God is a Mystery, but he is perceived as a mystery so close to us, so loving towards us, that we are drawn close to him. Sometimes words are helpful to us as we draw close; sometimes single phrases like 'God,' 'Love,' 'Jesus'; but there are also those precious moments when we abandon all use of words and draw close to God in a wordless silence, throbbing with love. Nothing needs to be said; nothing can be said. All is love, and all is God. We are caught up in this Reality, unable to speak, able only to respond with our heart in adoration and love.

It will be seen that the cloud of unknowing is by no means a barren experience for the heart. It is indeed frus-trating for that part of us which wants to explore and grasp and understand – our questing intellects. But the heart is not inactive while the intellect is being baffled. The heart is able to go on loving. As the mediaeval author said, it beats upon the cloud 'with short darts of longing love.' In fact it may be said that in some mysterious way, while our minds are brought up short by the baffling mystery of God, our hearts are not, but on the contrary are stimulated to love 'through' the cloud of unknowing. We love God all the more for being unable to grasp much about him except that he is present and loves us. This fact seems to me to be the distinctive truth about Christian mysticism. The mystery which is God baffles us in the mind so that we cannot formulate conceptual truths concerning God; but it does not stultify us in our hearts. We are stimulated and drawn to expand outwards towards God in love. Love increases and expands towards the Mystery and is not, apparently, handicapped by lack of comprehension. God can always be loved, whatever our state of comprehension of him. That is the heart of Christian prayer. 'By love may He be gotten and holden, but by thought never.'

In theological terms, this means that faith is always accompanied by hope and love. In the cloud of unknowing we live by faith that God is present and loves us. But we are not inactive or listless in this state. We strive to hope and to love the hidden God before us. We 'beat upon' that cloud with our hearts, and there is response from God. The cloud of unknowing is then to be not an obstacle to our loving God in prayer, but a God-sent purification. It cures us of the cosy tendency towards anthropomorphism. It raises our minds, in darkness, towards a true estimate of God, and so ensures that our love goes out to the real God, not a counterfeit divinity of our own making. The cloud of unknowing is a lesson in Truth. As the saints have said, it is a 'blessed night.' It is a stimulus in the soul towards union with God. The way human beings are made is that mystery stimulates our hearts in a way that fully understood reality does not. This is especially true in the field of religion. There, mystery acts as a sure guide towards Truth. As Arthur Balfour said, 'A god who is small enough for us to understand is not big enough for our needs.'

13

Towards Union

This is not an easy chapter to write, because it means talking about a degree of union with God which for most of us is in the future. We can, however, be guided by the writings of the mystics who have been where we have not yet been. They speak of a union with God which is like a log in a fire: the glowing log is so united with the fire that it *is* fire, while it, of course, remains wood. Mystics like to use metaphors because plain description breaks down. What is clear from their metaphors is that they envisage so close a union with God in prayer that in some true way the Christian soul can be said to be 'divinised.' It is not an absorption into the One whereby the individual loses all identity, which is the teaching of Indian mysticism. In Christian mysticism the individual remains completely himself and herself, but union with God is so close that they are caught up into the Trinity and begin to live the life of God himself. Comparisons with a log in the fire and white hot iron in a furnace are appropriate. Our personalities are transformed, not lost, in the furnace of God's love.

The union with God of advanced souls is not a new gift; it is merely the full realization of a gift which every Christian has: the gift of baptism. This is the distinctive Christian truth. Every baptized person, however much a sinner, is gifted with an unimaginably close union with God – a sheer gift, not our achievement. All baptized are made members of the Family of God, can call God 'Abba,' can know Christ to be brother, have the Holy Spirit within them, are temples of the Spirit. This sacramental union with God is in all Christians, and persists even through grave sin. The experience of prayer is to 'realize' this given union in such a way that we make it part of our daily life, make it actual in us. There is every difference between a baptized Christian who pays no attention to his gift and the one who responds to it with prayer. For the former the union with God is sacramentally real but dead; in the latter it is both real and alive, the most alive thing in his life. The log has begun to catch fire. Somewhere in between the dead Christian and the completely divinised Christian are the author and readers of this book. We are travelers on a road whose end is that complete union with God which the saints enjoyed. We should keep travelling and resist the temptation to be satisfied with any half-way house.

As we travel towards the prayer of union we find that prayer spills over into all our day and is not confined to special times. God and the soul are always present to each other, so their mutual exchange of love tends to go on all the time, with fewer interruptions, depending on the business which engages our surface selves. The time for prayer becomes now. This perpetually present opportunity to pray has been described in an unrivalled way by the seventeenth century French Jesuit Père de Caussade. In his letters and addresses to his charges (Visitation Sisters) he coined the phrase 'the Sacrament of the present moment.' The phrase has been remembered through the years as an apt description of the constant availability of prayer. Simple prayer needs no special time and place, nor any special spiritual apparatus. It is a question of responding to God's love generously as the minutes tick by. Each moment acts as a sacrament to us, bringing God's grace, God himself, into our life. We can be saints by simply treating each moment as a gift from God and spending it in his company and according to his will. When you try to do this you begin to understand the difference between a simple thing and an easy thing. Loving God is never *easy*. It becomes *simpler* the more we try it.

Simple prayer helps those who practise it not only to be sensitive to God's presence all the time, but also to be sensitive to the presence of God everywhere. We begin to find this world suffused with God's presence. We become sensitive to the Creator in and through his creation. Created things take on the aspect of symbols of their Creator. The sky above, the earth beneath our feet, stand for more than just what they are; they are seen as *sacraments* of God – as it were signposts pointing away from themselves to the Being who creates them and is to be found in them through his creative energy. The psalmist said that the Heavens proclaimed the glory of God. This is an ancient witness to this sacramental sensitivity. In the Middle Ages St Francis wrote his beautiful Canticle of Creatures in the same strain: blessed be God for the Sun, Moon, Fire, Water, Earth, all of which praise God by being themselves and bringing God's love to man. 'Praise be to thee, my Lord, for Sister Water,

who is very useful and humble, and precious and chaste.'
For St Francis, as for all non-puritans, the created world was
not an obstacle to loving God. It was the chief natural way
in which men and women were able to understand God
and rise towards him. Creation was a ladder, not an obstacle, in man's journey to heaven. In the last century Gerard
Manley Hopkins expressed this same Catholic sacramental
attitude in the beautiful lines:

> The world is charged with the grandeur of
> God.
> It will flame out, like shining from shook foil;
> It gathers to a greatness, like the ooze of oil
> Crushed.

The practice of constant prayer helps us to be aware of
God's presence in his creation and to commune with him
through it. That grandeur of God is always present and can
be discerned and adored in every place.

There is a sense in which the created world both hides
God and reveals him. It hides God, because it is material
and not spirit. An atheist can look at the beauties of the
world and not discern God's presence. God is hidden to
him. There is an additional sense in which this world hides
God, the sense outlined in the last chapter: no created thing
can possibly represent God because of the infinite gap
between Creator and creation. The infinite nature of God's
Truth and Goodness are hidden behind the instances of
finite truth and goodness in this world. There is no comparison. The mystics have always been acutely aware of this

incompatibility of God and Nature. They have therefore emphasised the necessary denials that have to be made when we use this-world language about God. A classic statement of this position is by St John of the Cross:

> '... among all creatures, the highest or the lowest, there is none that comes near to God or bears any resemblance to His Being. For, although it is true that all creatures have, as theologians say, a certain relation to God and bear a divine impress ...yet there is no essential resemblance or connection between them and God – on the contrary, the distance between their being and His Divine Being is infinite. Wherefore it is impossible for the (human) understanding to attain to God by means of creatures.'
>
> (Ascent of Mount Carmel, Book II, Ch. 8)

In other words, faced with the infinity of God, human beings are plunged into a cloud of unknowing from which they do not emerge in this life. This created, finite world hides God from us.

Nevertheless the mystics have also been the first to recognize that God's presence can be discerned in this world. Saints and poets have always celebrated this hidden, but discernible, Presence in the world. This is, in fact, no contradiction of the mystics' position, but a complementary truth. The mystics correctly point out that there is a gap of infinity between creation and Creator, but they are also insistent on the ubiquitous presence of God in creation. St John of the Cross was not only a rigorous theologian discerning the unknowability of God, but also the poet who hymned the beauty of God in this world and the novice master who led his novices out on to the Andalusian hillsides in order that they might more easily touch God among the beauties of Nature. The whole truth is that this world both hides God and reveals God at the same time. It is part of the mystery of our faith. God is hidden from the anthropomorphist who argues from this world to God too facilely (remember Yeats' poem). God is revealed to the eye of faith which discerns his presence in every creature, however small or great. This is the Catholic tradition, which has always sought to use the things of this world as symbols pointing to the Creator, especially in the liturgy. The more we allow prayer to develop in our lives along the lines outlined in this book, the greater chance we have of reaching God through liturgy and sacramentals. Prayer sensitises us to the presence of God in material things. It is the ally of sacramentalism.

From time to time in this book we have described prayer as a journey. At some place along the journey's road a Copernican revolution takes place in the relation between our souls and God. We pass from thinking of God as part of our life to the realization that we are part of his life. There is a shift in the centre of gravity. Copernicus, it will be remembered, was the astronomer who discerned that, contrary to appearances, the sun does not revolve round the earth, but the earth goes round the sun. The truth is the opposite of appearance. Something similar happens to us in our dealings with God. At first we cannot help placing God in our world. We are at the centre, God is in our circle. This is especially true if we have started from a position of agnosticism. Inevitably we are in the centre of our world, trying to make sense of it. Sense comes when we conclude that God exists and is our Creator. We find a place for God in our world, the most important place, the pivotal position, in fact. But even while we recognize that, we are still indefinably placing ourselves in the centre psychologically. We have found a place for God and Jesus Christ in our world. We begin to pray to him. Prayer also has found a place in our life.

Prayer leads us to Truth; so, sooner or later, the Copernican change takes place. Instead of granting God a place in my life, the realization dawns that he is Creator and has granted a place to me in his life. The world belongs to him, not me. I am in his world. I am an idea that he thinks up – not vice versa. I wake up in the morning to his creation. God is, in fact, at the centre. He is drawing me towards that centre, at his pace, in his time, according to his will. When this realization dawns, prayer is seen in a new, more relaxed way. It is seen not as a work, an achievement, but much more as a letting go, allowing God at the centre to do the work, becoming merely receptive to his work in us. We do not set out to master the road and make the journey on our own but, rather, allow God to draw us along the road by putting no obstacle (no 'buts') in the way. These are themes which have occurred in this book already.

To realize that God is at the centre of the universe drawing all created beings to him, that all initiative is with him, is to realize the central theme of the Bible. God takes the initiative; he loves us first. Jesus Christ is not merely a great human being making contact with God; he is the Son of God, descending into this world, made man for us. The

Holy Spirit is not a transformation of our inner selves under the influence of prayer, but the Spirit of God sent upon us and dwelling with us. That being so, it is well to make recognition of this in prayer. We should, in prayer, concentrate more upon God loving us than upon our poor efforts to love him. In our pre-copernican days we might be forgiven for concentrating in prayer upon our effort to reach God; but once the true state of affairs is realized, we should reverse the process: not reach out to contact God, but let go and allow God to contact us. God has already come to us in love. Prayer must be a reception of this unbelievable privilege; not striving but receiving should be the predominant mood of Christian prayer. He loves us. The best way for us to love him is to dwell on that marvellous fact and allow it to permeate our whole life.

A practical way in which to ensure that we recognize God's prior initiative in prayer is to take any of the movements of prayer which traditionally start with man and simply reverse them. Thus, I can begin prayer with the statement to God, 'I need you.' Turned round, the statement goes, 'God needs me.' This, believe it or not, since the New Testament, is true. The Lord needs me to be his hands, feet, mind, ears and voice in society. That is how he has established things: he acts through the members of his Body in every generation. He needs us; we are his contemporary disciples. Why not, then, in prayer recognize this? Dwell contemplatively on the fact in the phrase 'God needs me,' or better still 'You need me, Lord.' A very fruitful period of prayer can be spent simply dwelling on this, allowing its truth to seep into our inmost soul, responding to God in gratitude and love, till we are overwhelmed in a great communion of sharing with our divine Partner. As with the concept 'need,' so with other basic aspects of God's relationship to us: trust, thank, value, respect. Each of these can be reversed. You trust me; You thank me; You value me; You respect me. The principal effect of praying in this way, dwelling on God's attitude to me rather than my attitude to God, is a strong sense of unworthiness. To receive these attentions from the Creator-Lover does not puff me up with pride. It almost capsizes me in humility. This is an authenticating experience. Christians are, indeed, drawing close to God if they know themselves to be unworthy. They have joined company with the tax collector, not the pharisee, in Jesus' parable on prayer.

And so back to love. I love God, but – far more important – God loves me. We love each other. The prayer of union need move no further. It can stay there. Prayer becomes a celebration of this double gift of grace. When prayer has reached this stage, it has reached the utmost in simplicity. There is nothing more simple than two lovers surrendering to each other, in complete mutual trust, not needing words to express their love, just being together in love. Prayer has simplified to this state of mutual incandescence. The journey of prayer can end here. So can this book, because the chapter by chapter analysis of what goes on in prayer now gives way to the simple act of love, for which books are not needed.

Postscript

'In my Father's house are many mansions.' Luckily for all of us there is no one way to heaven, nor one type of Christian prayer. Each of us must find his or her best way of praying. I have written this book because experience tells me there are enough people who find the way of prayer here outlined congenial for me to be able to write a book about it; but I am far from thinking it is either the only way or even the best way. Recently, in an illness, I received a letter from a friend, an alcoholic down and out who has no religion and never goes to Church. She wrote: 'I hope my prayers helped you, although prayer is not one of my best habits. I really don't know how to pray, Father, so I just used to lie in bed at night and talk out loud hoping God was listening.' Perhaps that prayer was more pleasing to God than anything outlined in this book. It was simple and came from the heart. God does not ask more.